The Man
from the
USSR

and
Other Plays

VLADIMIR

NABOKOV

INTRODUCTIONS AND TRANSLATIONS
BY DMITRI NABOKOV

BRUCCOLI CLARK

HARCOURT BRACE JOVANOVICH, PUBLISHERS
SAN DIEGO   NEW YORK   LONDON

The Man
from the
USSR
and
Other Plays

WITH TWO ESSAYS ON THE DRAMA

©1984 by the Article 3b Trust Under the Will of Vladimir Nabokov
The Event ©1938 by Vladimir Nabokov; renewed 1966 by Vladimir Nabokov
Translations and Introductions ©1984 by Dmitri Nabokov

Requests for permission to make copies of any
part of the work should be mailed to:
Permissions, Harcourt Brace Jovanovich, Publishers,
Orlando, FL 32887.

Library of Congress Cataloging in Publication Data
Nabokov, Vladimir Vladimirovich, 1899-1977.
    The man from the USSR and other plays.

    Translated from the Russian.
    1. Nabokov, Vladimir Vladimirovich, 1899-1977 —
Translations, English. I. Nabokov, Dmitri. II. Title.
III. Title: Man from the U.S.S.R. and other plays.
PG3476.N3A26 1984   891.72'42   84-10862
ISBN 0-15-156882-0

Designed by Dalia Hartman

Printed in the United States of America

First edition

A   B   C   D   E

CONTENTS

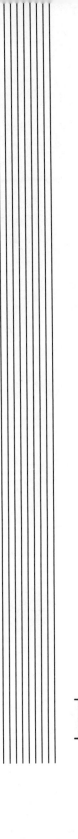

PLAYS

NABOKOV AND THE THEATRE

The relegation of writers to schools, movements, or social contexts, and the shrouding of their individuality in the mists of "influence" offer a fertile field for futile exercise. Father believed that the point of "comparative" literature was the exaltation of originality, not similarity. What mattered to him were the unique peaks, not the platitudinous plateau.

The hunt for leitmotifs and other echoes within a given author's oeuvre can also be an engrossing but pedestrian pursuit. Yet, certain special images and themes that flash and reverberate among Nabokov's peaks do merit comment, because they illuminate key facets of his works.

A fleeting refraction in many of Father's compositions, and a constant undercurrent in most of his dramatic writing, is the theatricality of all things, the ambiguity of the fictional reality, the deliberate glimpse through the fabric of the fictional world, into its wings, under its surface. The *butaforstvo*—"proppiness"—of what shows through can be (deliberately) a little shoddy, as the bowels of real theatres tend to be; or comforting, if it allows us respite from some unsettling nightmare being played out onstage; or eerie, when we think that the world may be a stage, but that here the stage becomes a world whose workings are not limited to the progression of the play or novel on its more obvious levels, and where even the reality of unreality comes into doubt.

The plays contain striking instances of such rippled reality: the "alternative" ending of *The Waltz Invention,* which is, in a sense, the protagonist's dream self-edited; the key scene of *The Event,* where for a fragile, magic moment a totally new dimension transforms the secondary characters into painted decorations and Troshcheykin and his wife into what are perhaps their real selves, reinforcing what a reviewer called the "somnambulistic atmosphere"; the last page of *The Grand-dad,* where the protagonist, the Passerby, suddenly finds himself questioning the authenticity of all that has supposedly occurred; Kuznetsoff who, in *The Man From the USSR,* is challenged by Marianna's barely camouflaged entreaty, "Why don't you say something?" and replies, "Forgot my lines"; Olga Pavlovna saying to Kuznetsoff, "I don't love you. There was no violin."— even though we all clearly heard one at the beginning of the act. Indeed, the fourth act's disordered, jumbled props and the "uneven gaps and apertures" through which peek the klieg lights of reality once removed (the film being shot in the offstage studio demystified by the exposure of its mechanical trappings) in themselves suggest the evanescent fragility of all that transpires before the audience. One is reminded of the haunting vacillations of reality in "A Visit to the Museum" and "Terra Incognita"; of the implication, with which *Invitation to a Beheading* concludes, that all the previous doings have been but theatrical artifice or someone's nightmare; and, of course, of the juxtapositions of worlds and realities in *The Real Life of Sebastian Knight, Ada,* and *Pale Fire.*

Closely related to the aura of a double reality is the double character, the so-called Nabokovian *doppelgänger.* The degree and the nature of the similarity between original and double — in the broad sense — may vary widely. The "pair" may consist of incidental characters with a modicum of physical resemblance, such as Meshaev One and Two in *The Event:* "... my brother and I were played by the same actor, only in the part of my brother he was good, and in mine he was bad." Or they may be near-twins in name only and belong to opposing camps within the world of the play, like the intimidating, off-stage Barbashin and the farcical Barboshin hired to foil him. The doubles may even exist only in portrait form: "... I painted two versions of him simultaneously on the sly: on one canvas as the dignified elder he wanted, and on the other the way *I* wanted him — purple mug, bronze belly, surrounded by thunderclouds" (a hint to the perceptive that there is something more to Troshcheykin than the rather unsympathetic façade he displays most of the time). Or there may be a dissimilar *doppelgänger,* an unwelcome companion: the executioner who travels by tumbrel with his victim to the scaffold in *The Grand-dad* and ominously foreshadows the grotesque M'sieur Pierre of *Invitation to a Beheading;* or a stand-in whose resemblance to the protagonist exists only in the latter's fantasy, as in *Despair.* The phenomenon of the double, in new and ingenious forms, was to play a crucial part in other novels as well: *The Real Life of Sebastian Knight,* the unfinished *Solus Rex* and its reincarnation in *Pale Fire,* and, of course, *Ada,* where the whole world is twinned. Nor let us forget "Scenes From the Life of a Double Monster" — a fragment of a larger, uncompleted work — and, of course, "The Original of Laura," where Flora's "exquisite bone structure slipped into a novel — became in fact the secret structure of that novel, besides supporting a number of poems."[1]

The voyage, in general; the scientific expedition, in

[1] © Article 3b Trust Under the Will of Vladimir Nabokov; unfinished and unpublished novel.

particular; and what is, in a sense, their antithesis — return to Russia — comprise another recurring arpeggio in Father's plays and other works. The idea of travel had tantalized him since childhood; the adventures of Phileas Fogg were among his most exciting early reading (as they were the young Luzhin's in *The Defense*). Ironically, the circumstances of exile would force him to travel more miles than Verne's hero had covered by choice, but that travel, too, was often food for inspiration: consider the émigrés of his stories and novels jouncing in their fourth-class compartments, or poor Pnin who does not know that he is on the wrong train, or Humbert's and Lolita's cross-country peregrinations. The conveyances and paraphernalia of travel had a romance all their own for Nabokov: witness the loving descriptions, autobiographical and fictional, of the veneered luxury expresses in their heyday, the lights of passing towns glimpsed upon lifting the leather blind of the Wagon-Lits, the trunks and *nécessaires* that accompanied the voyager. Witness also the elegant, appetizing, carefully selected baggage that survives Father in Montreux.

But the voyage with a special purpose had even more importance in Father's works. The thrill of the expedition always enchanted him. He confided to me once, late in life, that his life had been marvellously happy, his ambitions achieved, and most of his dreams realized. Two of his intense yearnings, however, did remain unfulfilled, and both were related to travel.

The first was to return to a non-Bolshevik Russia. Transformed by the kaleidoscope of his art, this idea finds its way, *inter alia*, into *Glory* (Martin's disappearance into the depths of the Soviet Union), "A Visit to the Museum" (until an orthographic detail makes the hero realize that his nightmarish traverse of the museum has transported him spatially but not temporally, and he has exited into contemporary, Soviet Russia), and, of course, *The Man From the USSR*.

Not only are Kuznetsoff's mysterious trips to the Soviet Union the central theme of the play, they are also the key to its whole atmosphere. Nabokov creates the illusion (as he does, in a different way, with the offstage Barbashin in *The Event*) that the real action is taking place elsewhere. This is true in a general sense: one has the feeling that the interpersonal relations around which the play itself revolves are overshadowed by much larger events occurring outside the stage, outside the theatre, outside the country. Kuznetsoff, in fact, sacrifices his sentiments and his married life in Berlin exile to his dangerous underground activities in Soviet Russia. In a more theatrical sense, as well, there is a curious contrast, in two of the acts, between the visible action and the physically larger, invisible happenings offstage (but which are, in fact, all only a backdrop for the onstage dialogue): the loud applause rewarding an inaudible lecture in the unseen auditorium; and, beyond the prop-cluttered stage, the film set, the thundering megaphone, the repeated takes of the uprising scene.

These instances of juxtaposition are curiously reminiscent of the conclusion of *Carmen* (offstage, Escamillo executing the bull to the public's cheers; onstage, the final, fatal exchange between Carmen and Don José in the deserted square outside the bullring). While *Carmen* was one of the operas Father liked, I would not go so far as to suggest that the parallel is intentional. Yet, not only is there a kinship between the theatrical tingles this effect generates in the two works, but one's attention returns to how we perceive, or are meant to perceive, different levels of reality or of illusion, with a new twist. What presumably happens or exists offstage is, in the simplest sense, as much an illusion as what we see played out before us. We know perfectly well that a stage set is not a real room or a real square, and we know just as well that there is no real bullring beyond the operatic *plaza*, no forest marching on Macbeth, no plunge to the pavement for Tosca from the crenel of the Castel Sant' Angelo. Yet there is also an intermediate theatrical reality: is the spectator expected to consider offstage structures or events *as real* as what transpires onstage? Of course the offstage sham may be shattered by the intrusion of real-life proppiness, as when a plumpish Floria Tosca bounces visibly from an overly resilient mattress just beyond the battlement. But it may also be *intended* to be perceived as nothing more than sham compared to onstage events, or at least to have its credibility questioned. One suspects that Nabokov, while suggesting momentous goings-on elsewhere, tips his hand to the spectator just enough to make him doubt the authenticity of the offstage lecture hall and movie set and of Kuznetsoff's cloak-and-dagger doings; of Barbashin's murderous intentions; of de Mérival's nightmarish recollection. Why is this done? The purpose—and effect—in these and other works of Nabokov's is to make the spectator's, or reader's, attention rebound from somewhat dubious offstage matters, *travel back*, and focus with increased intensity on the *visible* microcosm of the play, causing him to perceive it in a relief that would not otherwise be so vivid.

Theatrical works in general, when adapted to the screen, can cause a blurring of parameters. The cinema can even transport us from a rebuilt Globe Theatre to a realistic Battle of Agincourt, or from the grounds surrounding the Stockholm Opera House to a surreal recreation of Tamino's trials in a cinematic limbo somewhere beyond the actual stage. Although Nabokov acknowledged that certain works of his had a "cinematic slant,"[2] perhaps the *Lolita* screenplay

[2]Vladimir Nabokov, introductory note to "The Potato Elf," *A Russian Beauty and Other Stories* (New York: McGraw-Hill, 1973).

should not be included in a list of his theatrical works, as it is here, but should instead be the nucleus of a separate essay entitled "Nabokov and the Cinema."

Related to the "theme" of travel that has led us to the above considerations is that of the impoverished wanderer, a fictional relative of the Russian émigré who moves from place to place and job to job. De Mérival describes his roamings and occupations (in *The Grand-dad*), after he has escaped from the scaffold:

> In dank and melancholy London I
> gave lessons in the science of duelling. I
> sojourned in Russia, playing the fiddle at
> an opulent barbarian's abode. . . .
> In Turkey and in Greece I wandered then,
> and in enchanting Italy I starved.
> The sights I saw were many; I became
> a deckhand, then a chef, a barber, a tailor,
> then just a simple tramp.

His words are echoed by Fleming in *The Pole:*

> . . . . I've been a ship's boy and a diver,
> hurled my harpoon upon uncharted seas. Oh,
> those years of seafaring, of wandering,
> of longing. . . .

And, in *The Man From the USSR,* Fyodor Fyodorovich repeats the theme: "For over two years now I've enjoyed the most humble professions—no matter that I was once an artillery captain." More about the artillery captain later. Meanwhile, lest the reader misconstrue, let me make it clear that the point of these examples is not to spot some hypothetical symbolism or sublimation of the displaced person's lot.

Rather, it is to illustrate ways in which Father's creative process integrated this element—whose embryo may perfectly well be traceable to one aspect of his own émigré existence—into new and exciting combinations.

Nabokov's second unfulfilled longing was for a lepidopterological expedition to some exotic, uncharted region. Father had dreamed of the Caucasus, of Mount Elbrus, but, in later years, spoke most often of the Amazon. Again, what is fascinating here is not the simple association of ideas or the romanticizing of an unrealized fantasy, but the poetry of the pattern into which the thoughts were recombined to produce "Terra Incognita," the elder Godunov-Cherdyntsev's fantastic entomological journeys in *The Gift*, the prophetic space adventures of "Lance," and the touching mini-tragedy of *The Pole*.

This last work is a deliberately free synthesis of the Scott diaries. Nabokov's aim is not a precise journalistic reproduction but a rearrangement of elements into a concentrated interpersonal drama. Even the epigraph and its attribution—

"He was a very gallant gentleman"
(from Scott's notebook)—

are deliberately approximate. Scott did not write those words. They were left at the scene by the rescue expedition of 1912, led by E. L. Atkinson and A. Cherry Gerrard, which found the body. The exact wording was: "Hereabouts died a very gallant gentleman." This inscription was mentioned in chapter twenty-one of *Scott's Last Expedition*, of which Nabokov presumably saw the 1913 or 1915 edition in the South of France. The names, too, went through several generations of change and (except for Scott) never corresponded exactly to those of the actual expedition members.

Scott, himself, incidentally, was named "Bering" in an early manuscript version. The passage, near the end of the play, that is purportedly excerpted from Scott's diary was also deliberately adapted by Nabokov, as were many of the concrete details such as dates and distances. Even "Aurora australis" is changed to "Aurora borealis," I imagine because only the latter term was current in Russia at the time and had, by extension, come to represent the southern lights as well as their northern analogues. Significantly, the only two passages that retranslate into direct citations from Scott are the most touching lines of all: ". . . . I may well be some time. . . ," pronounced by Johnson in the play and Oates in Scott's diaries, while taking leave of the others with the conscious intention of dying in the snow in order to lighten their burden; and Scott's "I'm very sorry for my loyal companions." The lines

> It seems a pity, but I do
> not think I can write more. . . .

are the verbatim text of the final sentence of Scott's diary, except for his signature and the post scriptum, "For God's sake look after our people." I returned to the original text for "It seems a pity . . ." because Father unquestionably had made a literal Russian translation of these lines, even though he has Scott speak them to Fleming rather than read them from his notebook.

What had drawn Nabokov so strongly to these heroic explorers? Robert Falcon Scott was Britain at its best: unflinching in the face of danger, hardship, and pain, ever mindful of his companions' welfare, and tenacious to the end in his pursuit of a goal that was at once physical exploit and scientific adventure. His pure courage, his passion for the precision and poetry of nature, and his compassion for all that surrounded him were not unlike Father's own (and were later to be prototypical for the equally doomed Gregson of "Terra Incognita" and, to a degree, for the protagonist of "Lance"); Scott had a sense of humor as well, even in the direst circumstances (he addressed a final letter "To My Widow," a thought transferred by Nabokov to the fictional Fleming, who says: "Kingsley has a fiancée, almost a widow"). Fleming tries stoically to be—or seem—an optimist, to express a glimmer of hope even when calamity seems certain. Kingsley, in mortal delirium, dreams of bringing his fiancée a penguin who will be "smoo-smoo-smooth." (How Father loved saying *"gla-gla-gladen'kiy"* to me when I was very small, and what a delicious memory I have of those liquid Russian syllables!) Scott and Johnson, in the play, are based on real persons, with a change of name in the second case; Fleming and Kingsley less so (there was a Kinsey, but he was not a member of the final party). But no matter: here, again, the characters and events of the actual Scott expedition are only a point of departure. What counts is how they are refocused and recombined into the world and the poetry of this touchingly human drama. A writer, said Nabokov, must see "the marvels of this century, the little things . . . [and] the big things, like the sublime liberty of thought, and the moon, the moon. I remember with what tingles of delight, of envy, of anguish, I watched on the television screen the first floating footsteps of man in the talcum of our satellite and how I despised those who maintained it was not worth all those dollars to walk in the dust of a dead world."[3] (And I remember with what consternation I heard a writer very popular in some circles

[3] *Apostrophes,* French television, 1975. © Article 3b Trust Under the Will of Vladimir Nabokov. As in the other citations from *Apostrophes,* the translation from the French is mine.

announce, at a radical-chic dinner, that he hoped our astronauts would be marooned forever in space.)

Incidentally, Amundsen's victory in the race to the South Pole was, in a manner of speaking, not permanent. A couple of years ago the pole's exact locus was found to have shifted so that it had to be "rediscovered" and marked anew. That task was undertaken by the journalist Hugh Downs, with a strong assist from resident cartographer Loreen Utz of the U.S. Geographical Survey, for a segment of the television program *20/20* (whose programmers presumably realized that the pole has not lost its magnetism).

If, in *The Pole,* art in a sense deliberately imitates life, there is also a perfect case of the inverse process: life (unknowingly) imitating art. Not only was Nabokov's politico-military premise in *The Waltz Invention* prophetic of current issues and events, but the play recently had a hauntingly specific echo in the Italian press. We recall how Waltz threatened to explode a substantial and fairly distant mountain if his conditions were not met by the government, and then, in the "preliminary" or "dream" ending, proceeded to do so. Not long ago, a chauffeur appropriately named Antonio Carrus, residing in a village near Genoa, telephoned the major Italian news agency to predict a good-sized telluric tremor in distant Pozzuoli within the following twenty-four hours. After the event had duly occurred, he retelephoned to "claim" his quake, but would give no explanation of his prescience. "It might be a device, a discovery, a system," he said. "I shall explain only when the government begins to take me seriously." One can, in translation, almost hear Waltz speaking, so similar are the situation, the manner, and the words.

In addition to those already discussed, certain other Nabokovian themes, or subthemes, make preview appearances in the plays. In *The Grand-dad,* in particular, we find embryos of images that were to figure prominently in later works of Father's. I have already mentioned the executioner—the prototype of M'sieur Pierre—whom de Mérival, the Passerby, re-encounters in *The Grand-dad*. The play's surreal microcosm is curiously paralleled by the burgeoning nightmare of "A Visit to the Museum." The gradual inklings, the "strange associations" de Mérival begins to have as he is told how Grand-dad fondles the stems of lilies, to all of which he has given names "of duchesses, of marquesses," and how he has hurled Juliette's juice-incarnadined cherry basket into the stream are a chilling re-evocation of Revolutionary France akin to the protagonist's hallucinatory progression in "Visit" through the museum's rooms and into a post-Revolutionary Russia.

The burning scaffold that allows de Mérival to escape is a portent of the fires that will flicker or rage in other works. In *Lolita*, Humbert's whole destiny is changed by the conflagration that destroys the house where he would have lived. The burning of the "Baronial Barn" is the "contrived coincidence" that sets the scene for the crucial encounter between Van and Ada. Fire in *Transparent Things* spreads from theme to obsession to resolution.

As de Mérival flees from the blaze he plunges amid "torrents of smoke," "rearing steeds," "running people." One recalls Anton Petrovich's headlong tumble to salvation down the ever steepening, elder-overgrown slope in "An Affair of Honor." The "falling-through" theme, of course, was also to develop into the metaphysical traversal of solid objects, of levels of time and space, in *Pale Fire* and *Transparent Things*.

I stated at the outset of this introduction that particular recurring traits of Father's plays, as of his other works, merited discussion. Having examined them, however briefly, let us ponder where they lead.

As I suggested, there emerge certain fundamental considerations—two in particular—regarding Nabokov's work. The first is his fascination with transforming life into art on the chessboard of combinational possibilities. Just as he invented "scientifically possible" butterflies and "a new tree" (at Ardis),[4] so he recombined life into a fantastic but plausible reality. "I do not doubt," said Nabokov, "that there exists an intimate bond between certain images of my prose and the brilliant but obscure chess problems—magical enigmas—each of which is the fruit of a thousand and one nights of insomnia."[5]

Nabokov's point of departure may be pure conjecture (as in *Laughter in the Dark, Despair, Lolita, The Waltz Invention*), personal experience transformed (as in *Mary* and *The Gift*), a deliberate doubling of reality (as in *Ada, Pale Fire*, and, for a moment, *The Event*), a refraction of private fantasy (as in *The Defense, Glory, The Man From the USSR*), the personal adventures of others (as in "Terra Incognita," "Lance," *The Pole*), or history (as in *The Grand-dad* and, through a lens, in *Bend Sinister*). But his destination is a recombination of those materials into a kind of Hegelian triad (perceived by Nabokov as a spiral). The thesis of the triad (the basic plot, event, or idea) is dissected under the artist's microscope and made to reveal its mysteries and ambiguities, in which one perceives the antithesis (the *antiterra incognita*, the warp of time and space peeking through the fabric of the fiction). When superimposed and melded, the first two elements, or coils, of the triad yield the synthesis (the elements recombined into an original artistic whole).

"I discerned in nature the non-utilitarian delights that I sought in art," Nabokov said. "Both were a form of magic; both were a game of intricate enchantment and

---

[4] *Apostrophes.*
[5] *Apostrophes.*

deception."[6] Who but an artist or a deity can rearrange reality? It is a rare creative thrill. But such recombination would be a sterile exercise if performed for its own sake. The doubling, the ambiguity discussed earlier, is not simply a game. In considering the plays included in this volume, we have seen that it appears fleetingly in *The Man From the USSR,* gives an unexpected twist to *The Granddad,* and momentarily warps time and stage in *The Event.* Elsewhere, we are allowed a closer peek. In *The Gift,* for instance:

> The following day [(Alexander) Chernyshevski] died, but before that he had a moment of lucidity, complaining of pains and then saying (it was darkish in the room because of the lowered blinds): "What nonsense. Of course there is nothing afterwards." He sighed, listened to the trickling and drumming outside the window and repeated with extreme distinctness: "There is nothing. It is as clear as the fact that it is raining."
>
> And meanwhile outside the spring sun was playing on the roof tiles, the sky was dreamy and cloudless, the tenant upstairs was watering the flowers on the edge of her balcony and the water trickled down with a drumming sound.

If it is as clear as the fact that it is raining, it is not clear at all, for the rain is an illusion. Does that mean there might be *something?*

The sensation of fragile, twinned reality is more explicit in *Pale Fire.* While clinically dead, Shade sees a fountain, rather than the more common tunnel. His fascination with this

[6] "Vladimir Nabokov, The Great Enchanter," BBC Radio III, March 1982.

phenomenon leads him to track down a woman who, according to a newspaper item, has had the same experience. Only it turns out she had seen a *mountain,* and not a very convincing one at that: "Life Everlasting—based on a misprint." There follows a curious reversal of the Chernyshevski syllogism:

> I'm reasonably sure that we survive
> And that my darling somewhere is alive
> As I am reasonably sure that I
> Shall wake at six tomorrow, on July
> The twenty-second, nineteen fifty-nine,
> And that the day will probably be fine;
> So this alarm clock let me set myself,
> Yawn, and put back Shade's "Poems" on their shelf.

He is killed the same afternoon, shortly after having finished his poem. The reasonable certitude of his daughter's surviving in an afterworld is therefore just as precarious as that of his being alive the following morning. (The implication for Chernyshevski is: yes, there may be something; for Shade it is: no, chances are there is nothing.)

The deduction in Shade's case, however, is individual and not conclusive. Nabokov had a profound conviction, revealed in certain poems of his, in passages of *The Gift* and *Transparent Things,* and elsewhere, that he carried within him a knowledge of otherworldly truths to which others could not be made privy. It was a conviction that gave him a unique serenity (not unlike that of Scott) in the most trying circumstances, and of which he actually spoke publicly only in one interview. To the question, "Do you believe in God?" Father replied: "To be quite candid—and what I'm going to say now is something I never said before, and I hope it provokes a salutary little chill—I know more than I can express in words, and the little I can express would not have been expressed, had I not known more."[7]

Before *he* dies Shade does, for a moment, speak for Nabokov the artist. The essence of Shade's art is, as we have learned in Canto Three,

> ... Making ornaments
> Of accidents and possibilities.

Now, at the end of the fourth and final canto, he goes further:

> ... I feel I understand
> Existence, or at least a minute part
> Of my existence, only through my art,
> In terms of *combinational delight;**
> And, if my private universe scans right,
> So does the verse of galaxies divine
> Which, I suspect, is an iambic line.

The plays open a second, related, Nabokovian vista as well, an aspect of his works even less widely understood than the "combinational delights" just discussed.

To quote Martin Amis, Nabokov depicts his nastier characters with "such plangency . . . such moral unease," writing always more in their expiation, so that "the moral picture is always clear. . . . But to take the nastiness of the novels and impute it to Nabokov in any way seems to me futile. [It is] just part of what Nabokov is interested in, [this] possible nastiness of Art."[8]

---

[7]Interview with Alvin Toffler, *Playboy,* 11 (January 1964); reprinted in *Strong Opinions.* I have written in greater detail of this *potustoronnost'* (otherworldliness, sense of the hereafter) in "Translating with Nabokov," *The Achievements of Vladimir Nabokov,* edited by George Gibian and Stephen Jan Parker (Ithaca, N.Y.: Center for International Studies, Cornell University, 1984).
*Italics added.
[8] "Vladimir Nabokov, The Great Enchanter."

There are those who, like the late Edmund Wilson, with his imputations of *Schadenfreude,* consider Nabokov to have been a heartless puppeteer, aloof and indifferent to the misfortunes of his characters and of the world around him. Those who were closely acquainted with him know that nothing could be further from the truth. And for those who were not, a careful and sensitive reading of Nabokov reveals that he was (as Professor Denis Donoghue puts it) "extraordinarily tender toward broken things, maimed lives, and people who are completely ignorant of themselves."[9]

How pathetic are the elderly, evicted, not very pleasant Oshivenskis, in the last act of *The Man From the USSR.* Some of their attitudes may be suspect, and Oshivenski may detest that violin; but now they are penniless and are about to become homeless. Fyodor Fyodorovich arrives with the news that he has found them quarters at a different address. But the address is in Paradise Street, care of Engel. There is more than parody to "Paradise."[10] There is an echo here of Oshivenski's line immediately prior to Fyodor's arrival: "We'll meet in Paradise, God willing," and of an exchange that took place between the Oshivenskis a few minutes earlier:

MRS. OSHIVENSKI
And where are we supposed to go now? Oh my dear God. . . .

OSHIVENSKI
We'll move straight into the Kingdom of Heaven. At least there you don't have to pay the rent in advance.

---

[9] *Ibid.*

[10] To paraphrase Father's reference to the idyllic dotage of Van and Ada on *Apostrophes.*

These words also foreshadow Kuznetsoff's penultimate speech: "Olya, I'm going to the USSR so that you will be able to come to Russia. And everybody will be there. . . . Old Oshivenski living out his days, and Kolya Taubendorf, and that funny Fyodor Fyodorovich. Everybody." This suggests that they are all going to the same destination; that the Oshivenskis' new address will in fact be not Paradise Street, but Paradise, care of Angels; and that Kuznetsoff's voyage to the USSR (which will never again become "Russia") will be his last. The violin, that pitiful fourth-rate violin, plays again; Kuznetsoff pauses, recognizes the tune, and the tenderness that it has evoked and he has suppressed all through the play swells, on the final page, to the surface.

This whole, delicate work is unique, with its subtle play of nuance set in the special atmosphere of the Berlin emigration that Father knew so well. In addition to the bad violin there is Kuznetsoff's bad German, his colorful Russian, his basically rather amateurish secret agenting. There is the serene, resigned, desperately loving Olga Pavlovna, who is the only person to bring cash to the hopelessly indigent Oshivenskis. There is also the lighthearted Fyodor, whose statement (at the beginning of the play) that he "was once an artillery captain" is curiously echoed by Kuznetsoff in the final two lines:

OLGA PAVLOVNA
(pressing against him)
And you, Alyosha—where will *you* be?

KUZNETSOFF
(. . . somewhat mysteriously)
Listen—once upon a time there lived in Toulon an artillery officer, and that very same artillery officer—*(They leave.)*

Has he made some secret arrangement with Fyodor? Is Fyodor being groomed to march, like Napoleon (who, as an artillery officer, had lived in Toulon), on Russia? Will he be more successful? Or is Kuznetsoff simply confirming the omniscience he has already hinted at ("Everybody will be there. . . ."): I shall be in a place from where I shall *know,* and perhaps can even pull some strings.

Let us look again, through a different facet of the prism, at *The Event.* The key scene I have already once discussed may be surreal, but it is rich in very real compassion. The sometimes shrewish Lyubov' suddenly becomes human, gentle, understanding. Both she and Troshcheykin struggle to hold on to this aberration of space and time. The magic moment begins to slip away from both of them. She pronounces Tatiana's famous line from *Eugene Onegin:*

> Onegin, I was younger then,
> I daresay, and better-looking

and it is over. Money problems, the horrid maid Marfa, the fear of Barbashin all return to haunt them. But Lyubov' has had time to say (and nobody can take this away): "Our little son broke the mirror with a ball today. Hold me, Alyosha. Don't loosen your grip." The son is long since dead. The only balls around are those being used as props for the portrait of an extraneous child. And if anyone broke a mirror it was that child. Troshcheykin's grip loosens. The mad turn-of-the-century chess master Rubenstein preferred to play facing not his adversary but an empty chair and a mirror where he saw "his reflection or, perhaps, the real Rubenstein."[11] The mirror—

---

[11] *Apostrophes.*

and the spell—are broken. Which was the real Troshcheykin?

The Pole is a play with a more constant sense of pathos. The noble sportsmen-scientists are doomed. Kingsley (though it is Scott who, in other respects, foreshadows the later Gregson) is delirious. The bleak and unambiguous polar surroundings (subsequently, perhaps, deliberately recombined into the vacillating tropical trappings of "Terra Incognita") are a background for the sometimes surreal atmosphere created within the human soul. The polar nightmare, incidentally, is somehow reminiscent of the eerie visions and sensations reported by the early Everest mountaineers and even by Whymper, whose party saw fogbows of mysterious pattern on the Matterhorn (was it all caused by lack of oxygen and conditioning, or was it also the newness of the mountain adventure—and the polar one—to the human psyche?).

Finally let us turn again, for a moment, to *The Grand-dad*. Just as conjecture, adventure, and autobiographical experience were the raw materials for the combinational process elsewhere, here the *materia prima* is historical, while the central theme is a perennially current moral issue.

In an age when I, for one, find it hard to disapprove of capital punishment as a means of protecting our society from its more ruthless and demonstrably guilty members, Father steadfastly opposed it, as had his father Vladimir Dmitrievich Nabokov. It was Father's conviction that the remotest possibility of erroneously destroying even a single human life makes the death penalty fundamentally wrong. (I recall that his first concern upon seeing the bruised Oswald under guard was that he might have been arrested and beaten up unjustly.)

Nabokov makes his point, in *The Grand-dad*, more effectively than the most socially "involved" contemporary author. Granted that he was interested in the combinational possibilities of whatever subject he chose. But a viewpoint is a viewpoint, and true art is perhaps the most effective medium for its expression.

A condemned man who has escaped the guillotine through pure luck has a chance encounter, many years later, with his executioner. The latter is possessed by his need to complete the interrupted task: society has made him so, for new murderers are generated by the process of execution. He is obsessed by the urge to kill until his final moment. And here the artist takes over to explore the patterns the situation can create.

The creative process revealed in *The Grand-dad* is the necessary key, perhaps, for those who do not fully understand Nabokov, who criticize him for artistic aloofness, *Schadenfreude,* sterile gamesmanship, lack of concern, and so forth.

The executioner, so deeply tainted by the society in which he lived, reveals, like the despot Paduk in *Bend Sinister,* like the invisible manipulators of power in *Invitation to a Beheading,* a very profound involvement on Father's part. Who is to say that his involvement is less genuine or less effectual because it is refracted through the artistic prism?

Speaking of what Prof. Donoghue defines as Nabokov's "aesthetic relation to Russian literature and the tensions it exerts between art and propaganda,"[12] Alfred Kazin has pointed out that Nabokov perpetuates and develops the tradition of certain Russian formalist poets and scholars who were "very much concerned with art in a very special sense." It was not "art for art's sake" with the traditional con- notations, but rather "the idea of art as a new reality, . . . an idea Nabokov never lost. . . . He felt—in this he was a prophet—that. . . . Lenin was aiming at something very different from social reform or even social revolution. . . .

[12] "Vladimir Nabokov, The Great Enchanter."

[Nabokov] understood that Lenin wanted a separate reality. And we now know, for example, that one of the reasons for the absolute murderousness of totalitarianism is [the insistence]. . . . that communism is a separate reality that has entirely replaced capitalism [and] anyone who even [questions this] becomes an enemy of the system, so that we have an exclusive idea of salvation, which is quite frightful. And Nabokov understood this."[13]

It is too bad that the climate of the times and the limitations of Nabokov's audience prevented his prophecies from affecting the course of events. But if art is indeed reality, and a part of that reality is opinion on public matters, can one justly accuse Nabokov of lacking a social consciousness?

Nabokov identified beauty with pity, with the poetry and patterns of life itself. He detested brutality and injustice, whether toward a group or an individual. He had the same compassion for the victim of a crime as for someone unjustly punished for that crime. The outrage of a didactic tract, whether or not it purports to be literature and whatever its viewpoint, is hollow. The compassion of the true artist is sometimes poignant to the point of discomfort, which may be what bothers certain critics.

In translating the verse plays, I have deliberately tried for an accurate reproduction of the pentameter and the iambic foot wherever it was possible to reconcile them with reasonably natural speech patterns. It is true that Father's approach to the translation of poetry, as exemplified in his version of *Eugene Onegin* and other late translations of his own and others' verse, attained a literal purity wherein

[13] *Ibid.*

meter and (if present) rhyme were abandoned in the search for absolute accuracy of sense, nuance, and connotation. Where possible, however, he did strive for rhythm and alliteration. While Nabokov's more complex verse, with some of which I am grappling now, does dictate greater sacrifices to literality, I believe that, in the case of these wonderful, youthful verse compositions, the relative straight-forwardness of language would have led Nabokov to decide that there was no need, as a rule, to scrap the basic structure. Hence, while precision, of course, received absolute priority, I found it possible to preserve the overall metric scheme and the individual stresses with considerable accuracy (if one accepts, as in the Russian, the *ad libitum* use of an unaccented final syllable with the resultant feminine ending).

In the two prose plays there are certain deliberate departures from the original texts: in the case of wordplays, references, or special expressions that were untranslatable literally, or that, had they been translated, would have proved meaningless to the English-speaking reader or theatregoer.

In both the prose and the verse plays the possibility of performance has been kept in mind. I have tried to keep transliteration as straightforward as possible. "A" is of course sounded as in "ma," "e" as in "hey," "i" as "ee," "o" as something between "oh" and "aw" when stressed and as "uh" when not, "u" as in "put" with a bit of "boot," and "y" (except when used alone) is a purely auxiliary symbol denoting a diphthong sound, and is to be passed over as rapidly as possible. The soft-signed letters "l'" and "n'," in Russian, sound like the French "l" and "n" when the latter are followed by the vowel "i." The soft-signed final "v'" of "Lyubov'" is almost a French "f" when the latter is followed by "i." In addition to a one-time indication of stresses for Russian characters listed in the casts, stresses of diminutives as well as names and patronymics of persons mentioned in the text but not listed in Cast of Characters are indicated (in cases where there might be a doubt) at their first occurrence. The stress and transliteration business is purely utilitarian here, and has therefore been deliberately simplified.

It seems appropriate, in view of the variations that abound, to add that the author's name is stressed Vladímir Nabókov.

The four plays I have translated for this volume will soon be published by Ardis as part of a collection of Father's dramatic works in the original Russian.

DMITRI NABOKOV

CHRONOLOGY

A BRIEF CHECKLIST
OF DRAMATIC WORKS
BY VLADIMIR NABOKOV

(For more details regarding the history of the four plays included in this volume, see individual introductory notes.)

In the early 1920s Vladimir Nabokov wrote a couple of humorous playlets for a Russian variety theatre in Berlin; he also translated, for the same theatre, some imitation folk chestushki (a kind of Russian limerick).

Smert' (Death). A verse drama in two acts. Berlin, *Rul'*, 14 and 20 May 1923.

Dedushka (The Grand-dad). A verse drama in one act. Berlin, *Rul'*, 14 October 1923.

Skital'tsy (The Wanderers). A supposed translation of the first act of a play by the nonexistent English author "Vivian Calmbrood" (anagram). Berlin, *Grani*, 1923.

Agasfer. "A dramatic monolgue written as a prologue to a staged symphony" (VN's subtitle). Berlin, *Rul'*, 2 December 1923. Performed once in Berlin.

Traghediya Gospodina Morna (The Tragedy of Mr. Morn). A verse drama in five acts. Excerpt published Berlin, *Rul'*, 6 April 1924. Otherwise unpublished. Read by VN at a literary club meeting, early April 1924.

Polyus (The Pole). A verse drama in one act. Berlin, *Rul'*, 14 and 16 August 1924.

Chelovek iz SSSR (The Man from the USSR). Act one only: Berlin, *Rul'*, 1 January 1927. Staged in Russian in Berlin, 1926.

Sobytie (The Event). A "dramatic comedy" (VN's subtitle) in three acts. Paris, *Russkie zapiski (Annales russes)*, April 1938. Staged in Russian in various countries.

Izobretenie Val'sa (The Waltz Invention). A drama in three acts. Paris, *Russkie zapiski*, November 1938. English translation by Dmitri Nabokov (New York: Phaedra, 1966); Dutch and Spanish translations. Staged in Russian and English in various countries.

Rusalka (The Water Nymph). "A concluding scene to Pushkin's

Rusalka" (VN's subtitle). New York, *Novy zhurnal (The New Review)*, No. 2, 1942.

Lolita: A Screenplay. New York: McGraw-Hill, 1974. Used only in part for the 1962 Kubrick-Harris film based on the novel.

Note: This chronology is based partly on the same source material as sections of Andrew Field's *Nabokov. A Bibliography* (New York: McGraw-Hill, 1973), which, though flawed, was of some help in this instance.

The Man
from the
USSR

DRAMA IN FIVE ACTS

INTRODUCTORY NOTE

The Man From the USSR was written in Berlin in 1925-1926. The first act only was published in *Rul'* on 1 January 1927. The entire play had been staged by a Russian theatrical company called *Gruppa* (The Group) at the Grotrian-Steinweg Saal in Berlin in 1926. For the present translation I have used the manuscript text preserved in one of my grandmother's albums.

NB: "Kuznetsoff" is a deliberate departure from normal transliteration.

CAST OF CHARACTERS[1]

Alexéy Matvéyevich (Alyósha) Kuznetsóff, a businessman
Ólga Pávlovna (Ólya), his wife
Víctor Ivánovich (Vítya) Oshivénski, proprietor of a small
  tavern, former landowner
Yevghénia Vasílyevna (Zhénya, Mrs. Oshivenski), his wife
Mariánna Sergéyevna Tal', a film actress
Lyúlya, her friend
Baron Nikoláy Kárlovich (Kólya) Táubendorf, waiter,
  former officer
Fyódor Fyódorovich, waiter, former officer
The Assistant Director
émigrés, film extras, stagehands, and passing legs

---

[1] The Cast of Characters was provided by the author, with the exception
of one name, omitted in his mother's transcription, and reinstated here.
Stresses (´) are provided for the readers' and the performers' convenience.

ACT ONE

Small tavern in a basement. In the back, a narrow horizontal window—a strip of glass spanning almost the entire length of the room. Since the window is at sidewalk level, only the legs of passersby are visible. On the left*, a door, curtained with blue cloth; its threshold is level with the bottom edge of the window, and a visitor must descend six blue steps to reach the basement. To the right of the window, an obliquely situated bar; behind it, along the right wall, shelves with bottles and, downstage of them, a low door leading into the cellar. The proprietor has evidently attempted to give the tavern a Russian atmosphere by means of blue babas and peacocks painted on the rear wall above the strip of window, but his imagination has stopped there. It is about nine o'clock on a spring evening. Life has not yet begun in the tavern: tables and chairs stand haphazardly; here and there the angular white shapes of spread tablecloths strike the eye. Fyodor Fyodorovich, a waiter, is bent over the bar, arranging fruit in two baskets. There is an evening dimness in the tavern, and that makes Fyodor Fyodorovich's face and his white smock seem especially pale. He is about

---

* Left and right as seen by the audience: the reverse of stage left and stage right. True of subsequent stage directions as well.

twenty-five, with fair hair slicked down very thoroughly. His profile is angular, and his movements are not devoid of a certain careless swagger. Victor Ivanovich Oshivenski, owner of the tavern, a slightly chubby, neat old man with a short gray beard and a pince-nez, is nailing to the wall, to the right of the window, a large white sheet, on which one can distinguish the inscription "Gypsy Chorus." From time to time legs pass from left to right and from right to left in the strip of window. They stand out against the yellowish background of evening with a two-dimensional clarity, as if cut out of black cardboard. If one compared the action onstage to music, these silhouettes would serve as black quavers and semiquavers. Of course they do not pass continuously, but at considerable intervals. From the opening curtain until the moment when Fyodor Fyodorovich lowers the blinds at Kuznetsoff's appearance, only ten pairs of legs pass, of which two cross from opposite directions, two follow each other in rapid succession, and the rest pass individually.

Oshivenski pounds, for a certain length of time, then drops his hammer with a spasm of pain.

OSHIVENSKI
Damn! . . . Right on my thumbnail. . . .

FYODOR FYODOROVICH
Mustn't be so careless, Victor Ivanovich. That really hurts, doesn't it?

OSHIVENSKI
I'll say it does. . . . The nail will probably come off.

FYODOR FYODOROVICH
Here, let me hammer. The lettering is well done, though, if I

do say so myself. I admit I tried very hard. Those letters are a dream.

OSHIVENSKI

These gypsies are just an extra expense anyway. They won't
bring in any new customers. It's only a matter of days before
my little place . . . what do you think — maybe I should soak it
in cold water?

FYODOR FYODOROVICH

Yes, that helps. There, it's ready! Right where it strikes the
eye. The effect isn't bad at all.

OSHIVENSKI

. . . It's only a matter of days before my little place folds. And
that will mean running around this damned city of Berlin
again, searching, trying to think something up. . . . And meanwhile, like it or not, I'm pushing seventy. And how tired I am,
how very tired. . . .

FYODOR FYODOROVICH

I think it'll look better this way: green grapes with the
oranges, red with the bananas. Simple and appetizing.

OSHIVENSKI

What time is it?

FYODOR FYODOROVICH

Going on nine. I suggest we arrange the tables differently
today. Anyway, next week when the gypsies get going we'll
have to clear a space over there.

OSHIVENSKI

I'm beginning to think that there is a hidden flaw in the

concept itself. At first it seemed to me that this kind of nighttime tavern, a basemènt place something like the "Stray Dog," would have a particularly attractive atmosphere. The very fact that legs flit by on the sidewalk, and that special kind of—what's the word—oh, you know, coziness, and so forth. Don't crowd them together too much, though.

FYODOR FYODOROVICH

No, I think it works out nicely like this. Here's a tablecloth that needs changing. Wine got spilled on it last night. Turned it into a regular map of the world.

OSHIVENSKI

I'll say. And the laundering doesn't come cheap, either. Anything but. That's a perfect example: it would probably have been better to open up not a tavern but just a café, a little restaurant, something very ordinary, and don't you sniff with indifference, Fyodor Fyodorovich.

FYODOR FYODOROVICH

Why should I sniff? Sniffing only creates drafts. Don't you worry, Victor Ivanovich, we'll make a go of it somehow. Personally I don't care what I do, and I even think it's fun being a waiter. For over two years now I've enjoyed the most humble professions—no matter that I was once an artillery captain.[2]

OSHIVENSKI
What time is it?

FYODOR FYODOROVICH
As I told you, it's close to nine. Soon they'll start gathering.

---

[2] Like Napoleon. For performance, this reference may be included in the speech if it is deemed unclear.

Those legs are heading here.
(There appears, in the strip of window, a pair of legs, which first cross from left to right, then stop, then go in the opposite direction, then stop again, then change direction again. They belong to Kuznetsoff, but are seen in silhouette form, i.e., two-dimensional and black, like black cardboard cutouts. Only their outline is reminiscent of his real legs, which [in gray pants and sturdy, tan shoes] will appear onstage together with their owner two or three speeches later.)

OSHIVENSKI

And one fine day nobody will gather at all. Listen, old chap, pull down the blind and turn on some lights. Yes . . . one fine day. . . . A colleague of mine in the tavern business—what's his name . . . Meyer—was telling me everything was going fine, his place was flourishing—then, suddenly, what do you know: nobody shows up. . . . Ten o'clock, eleven, midnight—nobody. . . . Matter of chance, of course.

FYODOR FYODOROVICH

I told you those legs were coming here.
(The blue cloth covering the door begins to bulge.)

OSHIVENSKI

A matter of chance all right, but an amazing one. Nobody came at all that whole night.
(Pushing aside the cloth, Kuznetsoff appears and pauses on the top step. He is dressed for travel: gray suit, no hat, tan raincoat draped over his arm. He is a man of average height with an unprepossessing clean-shaven face, with narrowed myopic eyes. His hair is dark and slightly thinning at the temples, and he wears a polka-dot bow tie. At first sight it is hard to tell if he is a foreigner or a Russian.)

FYODOR FYODOROVICH
(jauntily)
Guten abend.
*(He turns on the lights and lowers the blue blinds. The passing legs
disappear from view.)*

OSHIVENSKI
(in a low-pitched drawl)
Guten abend.

KUZNETSOFF
(cautiously negotiating the stairs)
Hello. It's no good having those stairs going right down from
the door.

OSHIVENSKI
Beg pardon?

KUZNETSOFF
It's treacherous—particularly if the customer is already
tipsy. He'll come crashing down. You'd better do something
about it.

OSHIVENSKI
Well, you know, there's not much you can do—after all, this
is a basement, and if I start setting up a platform there—

KUZNETSOFF
I was told that Baron Taubendorf is working as a waiter here.
I'd like to see him.

OSHIVENSKI
That's absolutely correct—he's already been with me for two
weeks. Maybe you'd like to sit down—he should be here any

minute. Fyodor Fyodorovich, what time is it?

KUZNETSOFF

I don't feel like waiting. You'd better tell me where he lives.

FYODOR FYODOROVICH

The Baron comes in at nine on the dot. For the opening curtain, so to speak. He'll be here in a moment. Do sit down. Sorry about the boxes of nails on the chair. . . .

KUZNETSOFF

(sits; a box falls down)
Didn't see it.

FYODOR FYODOROVICH

Don't worry, I'll pick them up. *(drops to one knee in front of Kuznetsoff and begins picking up the scattered nails)*

OSHIVENSKI

Some people find a certain charm in the fact that you enter by descending a flight of stairs.

KUZNETSOFF

All these props are no use. How's business? Bad, I suppose?

OSHIVENSKI

Not so good. . . . Not many Russians around—well-to-do ones, I mean; there's no shortage of poor ones, of course. As for the Germans, they have their own pubs, their own habits. So we struggle along as best we can. At first it seemed to me that the idea of a basement tavern . . .

KUZNETSOFF

Well, right now your tavern's pretty empty. How much are your expenses?

OSHIVENSKI

On the high side, to be quite frank. I rent it, but you know how that goes — if I needed a basement for storage, there'd be one price, this way it's another. And when you add on —

KUZNETSOFF

I'm asking you for an exact figure.

OSHIVENSKI

One hundred twenty marks. Plus tax, and what a tax. . . .

FYODOR FYODOROVICH
(peeking behind the blind)
And here's the Baron!

KUZNETSOFF
Where?

FYODOR FYODOROVICH
I can tell by his legs. Remarkable thing, legs.

OSHIVENSKI

Besides, I had some bad luck with the wine. They got me to buy a batch that was supposed to be a bargain. Instead —
(Taubendorf enters. He is wearing a hat but no coat. He is thin, has a clipped mustache, and is dressed in a worn but still elegant dinner jacket. He pauses on the top step, then comes rushing down.)

KUZNETSOFF
(getting up)
Greetings, Kolya.

TAUBENDORF
I'll be damned — great to see you! After all these winters, all

these summers. More winters than summers. . . .

KUZNETSOFF

No, it's only been eight months. Hello, pal, how are you?

TAUBENDORF

Wait, let's have a look at you. . . . Victor Ivanovich, treat him well — he's a dear friend.

OSHIVENSKI

Off we go to the wine cellar, Fyodor Fyodorovich.
(Oshivenski and Fyodor Fyodorovich go out the door on the right.)

TAUBENDORF
(laughing)
My boss is a bit on the deaf side, but he's a man of gold. All right, Alyosha, hurry, while we're alone, tell me everything.

KUZNETSOFF

What's wrong with you — why all the excitement?

TAUBENDORF

I want to hear the news. . . . Are you here for long?

KUZNETSOFF

Hold on a moment. I just came from the station, and first of all I want to know . . .

TAUBENDORF

This is incredible! You've seen and done God only knows what, and God only knows what danger you've been in . . . suddenly you reappear and, as if nothing had happened, there's not a word out of you.

KUZNETSOFF

(sitting down)

You'd probably like to see me wearing an operetta sword and gold braid. That's not what it's all about. Where is my wife living now?

TAUBENDORF

(standing in front of him)

Fifty-three Hegel Street, Pension Braun.

KUZNETSOFF

I see. I rode over from the station to where she lived last time I was here. They didn't know her address. Is her health all right?

TAUBENDORF

Yes, she's fine.

KUZNETSOFF

I wrote her twice. Once from Moscow and once from Saratov. Did she get my letters?

TAUBENDORF

Yes, sir. The post office forwarded them.

KUZNETSOFF

And how is her financial situation? Do I owe you anything?

TAUBENDORF

No, she had enough to tide her over. She lives very modestly. Alyosha, I can't stand it any longer — tell me — how is it going?

KUZNETSOFF

Right. . . . address, health, money. . . . What else was there?

Oh, yes—She hasn't gotten herself a lover, has she?

KUZNETSOFF

TAUBENDORF
Of course not!

KUZNETSOFF
Too bad.

TAUBENDORF
Besides, that's a shocking question. . . . She's such a darling, your wife. I'll never understand how you could have left her. . . .

KUZNETSOFF
Use your head, sweetheart, and you'll understand. One other question: why are you wearing eyeliner?

TAUBENDORF
(laughing)
Oh, that's makeup. Very hard to get off.

KUZNETSOFF
What have you been up to today?

TAUBENDORF
Extra work.

KUZNETSOFF
What does that mean?

TAUBENDORF
At night I'm a waiter here, and during the day I'm a film extra. Right now they're shooting an idiotic picture about Russia.

KUZNETSOFF

Now let's get down to business. Everything is going fine. Comrade Gromov, whom by the way I'll see at the Soviet Mission, has been hinting to me about a promotion, which, naturally, is very gratifying. But, as before, I am short of cash. This must be remedied: I have to meet with a whole lot of people here. Now listen—day after tomorrow Werner is coming in from London. You will give him this...and this.... *(hands him two letters)*

TAUBENDORF

Alyosha, remember what you promised me last time?

KUZNETSOFF

I do. But that's not necessary for now.

TAUBENDORF

But I'm only a pawn. My job consists of such trifles. I'm not kept informed of anything. You refuse to tell me anything. I don't want to be a pawn. I don't want to play postman. You promised, Alyosha, that you would take me to Russia with you....

KUZNETSOFF

Don't be a fool. So, you'll give this to Werner, and also tell him—
(Oshivenski and Fyodor Fyodorovich return with bottles.)

TAUBENDORF

Alyosha, they're coming back....

KUZNETSOFF

...that the price of nails is stable.... And be at my place tomorrow at eight. I'm at the Hotel Elysium.

TAUBENDORF

What's tomorrow, Tuesday? Yes—fortunately tomorrow is my night off.

KUZNETSOFF

Splendid. We'll have a chat, and then we'll go look for some chicks.

OSHIVENSKI

Baron, give us a hand here. Soon people will start coming. *(to Kuznetsoff)* May I offer you some cognac?

KUZNETSOFF

Many thanks. I won't refuse. How does one get to Hegel Street from here?

OSHIVENSKI

It's right nearby: turn right, go three blocks, and you're there.

FYODOR FYODOROVICH
(pouring the cognac)
Hegelkinsky. . . .

TAUBENDORF

Victor Ivanovich, I think you're acquainted with Mr. Kuznetsoff's wife.

KUZNETSOFF

Allow me to introduce myself.

OSHIVENSKI

Oshivenski. *(They shake hands.)* Ouch! Excuse me, but I just hit my thumb with a hammer.

KUZNETSOFF

Oh, so you're left-handed?

OSHIVENSKI

Yes, of course I know her. We met at Easter. My wife, Yevghenia Vasilyevna, and she are great friends.

TAUBENDORF

Listen, how did you guess that Victor Ivanovich was left-handed?

KUZNETSOFF

Which hand do you usually hold a nail with? You're a real whiz kid. . . .

OSHIVENSKI

So you've been out of town?

KUZNETSOFF

Yes, out of town.

OSHIVENSKI

Warsaw, wasn't it? I think that's what Olga Pavlovna said. . . .

KUZNETSOFF

Yes, I visited Warsaw too. To your health.
(Marianna enters. She is wearing a light-gray tailored dress, and has short hair. Her legs and lips immediately identify her as a Russian. She walks with a loose gait.)

TAUBENDORF

Your obedient servant, Marianna Sergeyevna.

MARIANNA

You're an awful stinker, Baron. How come you didn't wait for me? Moser gave me a lift back in his car, and there was room for you, too.

TAUBENDORF

Marianna dear, I was a wreck after the shooting—what with the klieg lights and the yelling and everything. And I was hungry.

MARIANNA

You could have warned me. I looked all over for you.

TAUBENDORF

I beg your forgiveness. The humble extra begs the forgiveness of the film star.

MARIANNA

No, I'm very hurt. And please don't think the only reason I dropped in here was to tell you that. I need to make a phone call. *Guten abend,* Victor Ivanovich.

OSHIVENSKI

It's time you stopped getting lovelier, Marianna Sergeyevna: the thing could assume monstrous proportions. Mr. Kuznetsoff, this famous film starlet lives in the same modest boardinghouse as your wife.

MARIANNA

How do you do. *(nods to Kuznetsoff)* Victor Ivanovich, may I use your phone?

OSHIVENSKI

To your heart's content.
(Marianna crosses to the door on the right, near which the telephone is located.)

FYODOR FYODOROVICH

I guess nobody wants to say hello to me.

MARIANNA

Oh, excuse me, Fyodor Fyodorovich. By the way, show me what I have to do to call out from here.

FYODOR FYODOROVICH

First you have to press the nipple — here, this little red button.

KUZNETSOFF
(to Taubendorf)
Kolya, that's what I call a real looker. Or else, as they also say, a classy broad. *(laughs)* An actress, is she?

TAUBENDORF

Yes, she and I are working together in a film. Only, I play the crowd and get ten marks, and she plays the Other Woman and gets fifty.

MARIANNA
(into the phone)
Bitte, drei und dreissig, eins null.

KUZNETSOFF

Of course that isn't the lead?

TAUBENDORF

No, the Other Woman always makes less than the heroine.

KUZNETSOFF
Last name?

TAUBENDORF

Tal'. Marianna Sergeyevna Tal'.

KUZNETSOFF

It's convenient that she lives in the same boardinghouse. She can take me there.

MARIANNA
(into the telephone)
Bitte, Fräulein Rubansky. Oh, it's you, Lyulya. I didn't recognize your voice.

FYODOR FYODOROVICH

I guess we can turn on the rest of the lights, Victor Ivanovich. Soon it'll be ten o'clock.

OSHIVENSKI

If you want. . . . I have a feeling nobody will come tonight.
(Fyodor Fyodorovich turns on the remaining lights.)

MARIANNA
(into the phone)
Nonsense. Where did you hear that? We finish shooting in a week—they're in a terrible rush. Yes.

TAUBENDORF

Alyosha, forgive me if I ask: aren't you the least bit anxious to see your wife?

MARIANNA
(into the phone)
Oh, he's such a pest. . . . What did you say? No, of course not.

I can't tell you now — I'm not alone here. Ask a question, and I'll answer. Oh, you're so silly — of course not. Yes, he usually drives himself, but not today. What did you say?

KUZNETSOFF

Actually, what do you care whether I'm anxious or not? Is she married?

TAUBENDORF

Who?

KUZNETSOFF

This one here. . . .

TAUBENDORF

Oh, this one. . . . Yes, I think so. She lives alone, though.

MARIANNA
(into the phone)

What a rotten thing! Did he really say that? *(laughs)* What? You have to hang up? Who's keeping you from talking at your end? Oh, I see, I see . . . *(with a lilt)* Auf wiederse-e-ehn.

KUZNETSOFF
(to Marianna)

You didn't talk very much. I thought it would take longer.

OSHIVENSKI
(to Marianna)

That'll be twenty pfennigs. Thank you. First cash that's come in today.

MARIANNA
(to Kuznetsoff)

And why did you think it would take longer?

KUZNETSOFF
Can I buy you a drink?

MARIANNA
What do you take me for, a bar girl?

FYODOR FYODOROVICH
Bar the bar girls.

KUZNETSOFF
If you don't want to you don't have to. *(to Taubendorf)* So I'll see you tomorrow, Kolya. Don't be late.

MARIANNA
(to Kuznetsoff)
Wait—let's sit down over there. I guess I can spare a minute.

FYODOR FYODOROVICH
The huge hall was inadequate for the enormous crowd.

OSHIVENSKI
You know what, Fyodor Fyodorovich, be a good chap and turn off the big lamps, would you? It's just an added expense.
(He sits in a wicker chair by the bar and listlessly leafs through a newspaper. Then he grows pensive and yawns a couple of times.)

TAUBENDORF
(approaching the table, situated downstage, where Marianna and Kuznetsoff are seated)
What is your pleasure? Some wine? A liqueur?

KUZNETSOFF
I don't care. Make it a cherry brandy.

MARIANNA
How odd: Olga Pavlovna never told me anything about you.

KUZNETSOFF
Good for her. Are you free tomorrow night?

MARIANNA
Do you really care to know?

KUZNETSOFF
In that case I'll meet you at ten o'clock sharp in the hall of the Hotel Elysium. And bring Lyulya along too. I'll be with Taubendorf.

MARIANNA
You're crazy.

KUZNETSOFF
And the four of us will go to some racy little spot.

MARIANNA
You're absolutely unbelievable. One might think you've known me and my girl friend for a hundred years. I should never have had that liqueur. When I'm so tired, I have no business drinking liqueurs. And I am terribly tired. . . . These shooting sessions. . . . And my part is the most demanding one in the whole film. The part of a Communist woman. Abominably difficult part. Have you been in Berlin long?

KUZNETSOFF
About two hours.

MARIANNA

And imagine, today I had to repeat the same scene eighteen—yes, eighteen times. Of course it wasn't my fault. It was because of Pia Mora. Of course she's very famous, but, between you and me, if she is playing the lead, it's only because . . . well, in a nutshell, it's because she's making it with Moser. I watched her seethe when she saw I was better than her. . . .

KUZNETSOFF

(to Taubendorf, over his shoulder)
Kolya, tomorrow we're all going out to have a good time. Okay?

TAUBENDORF

Whatever you say, Alyosha. I'm always ready.

KUZNETSOFF

Then it's settled. And now—

MARIANNA

Baron, could you find my handbag for me? I left it somewhere by the phone.

TAUBENDORF

At your service.

KUZNETSOFF

And now I want to tell you something. I like you a lot, especially your legs.

TAUBENDORF

(returning with the handbag)
Here you are.

MARIANNA

Thank you, my dear Baron. I'd better go. The atmosphere is getting too romantic. . . . The dim lighting and all . . .

KUZNETSOFF

(getting up)

Romance is the spice of life. Let's go. You have to show me the way to the Pension Braun.

FYODOR FYODOROVICH

Where's your hat, Mr. Kuznetsoff?

KUZNETSOFF

Never use one. Oh-oh—the boss is snoring. I won't disturb him. Good-by, Fyodor Fyodorovich—that's right, isn't it? Kolya, how much do I owe you?

TAUBENDORF

A mark and a half. Including gratuities. See you tomorrow, Marianna dear. See you tomorrow, Alyosha. Eight-thirty.

KUZNETSOFF

Don't bungle things, sweetheart. I said eight.
(Kuznetsoff and Marianna leave.)

FYODOR FYODOROVICH

(lifting the edge of the window blind and looking out)

Amazing thing, legs.

TAUBENDORF

(yawning)

Oh-hoh. Doesn't look good. I guess no one is going to come.

Come on, let's have a game of twenty-one.

FYODOR FYODOROVICH
Oh well—why not.
(They sit down at the same table where Kuznetsoff and Marianna were sitting and start playing. Oshivenski is sleeping. It is rather dark.)

CURTAIN

ACT TWO

A room. On the left a window giving on the courtyard. Door in rear wall, opening on a corridor. In the left corner, a green-colored settee with a green egg-shaped cushion. Next to it, a small table with a round lamp. By the right wall, behind a green screen, a bed: the only part of it visible to the spectator is one of the metal knobs at its foot. In the center, a round table with a lace doily. Near it, in an armchair, sits Olga Pavlovna Kuznetsoff, embroidering a silk chemise. She is wearing a very simple, not quite fashionable dark dress: it is more ample and longer than the current style. Her face is young and soft; there is something girlish about her gentle features and smooth hairdo. The room is an ordinary room in an ordinary Berlin boardinghouse, with aspirations to bourgeois comforts: a pseudo-Persian carpet; two mirrors, one in the door of a puunchy wardrobe against the right wall, the other an oval one on the back wall. In all of this there is a kind of unpleasant puffy rotundity — in the armchairs, the green lampshade, the outline of the folding screen, as if the room had developed in concentric circles, frozen motionless over there in the form of a pouf, over here in that of an enormous plate stuck to the peony design of the wallpaper and giving birth to several smaller ones all over the back wall. The window is ajar — it is a bright, spring afternoon. A very badly played violin is audible outside. Olga Pavlovna, busy with her embroidery, listens now and then and smiles. The violin gives one last whine, sobs and falls silent. A pause. Then, beyond the door, Kuznetsoff's voice inquires, "Wo ist mein[3] Frau?" and the maid's irritable voice replies, "Da—nächste Tür."

OLGA PAVLOVNA
(drops everything, runs to the door, opens it)
Alyosha, I'm in here. Come here.

KUZNETSOFF
(enters, with his raincoat over his arm)
Hello. What do you think you're doing sitting in someone else's room?

OLGA PAVLOVNA
Marianna doesn't mind. And they're doing my room—I got up late. Put down your coat.

KUZNETSOFF
And where did she go?

OLGA PAVLOVNA
I really don't know. Off somewhere. I don't know. Alyosha, it's already been four days, but I simply can't get used to the idea that you're in Berlin, and come to visit me—

KUZNETSOFF
(walking to and fro, picking up a framed photograph from a side table)
It's hot in here and it reeks of perfume. Who is this character?

---

[3] *Mein* is deliberately incorrect; Kuznetsoff's German is not very good.

OLGA PAVLOVNA

—that I no longer have to wait for your letters, wonder where you are and whether or not you're alive. . . .

KUZNETSOFF

Her husband, is it?

OLGA PAVLOVNA

Yes, I think so. I don't know him. Sit somewhere. You can't imagine how enormous Russia seems to me when you disappear into it. *(laughs)*

KUZNETSOFF

Nonsense. Actually I only stopped by for a moment. I still have loads of things to do.

OLGA PAVLOVNA

Oh, sit down for a little while. Please. . . .

KUZNETSOFF

I'll drop by to see you again later. And I'll take a nap.

OLGA PAVLOVNA

Can't you stay ten minutes? I have something to tell you. Something very amusing. But I'm a little embarrassed because I didn't tell you as soon as you arrived. . . .

KUZNETSOFF

What is it?

OLGA PAVLOVNA

Last Monday about nine o'clock—the same day you arrived— I was walking home and saw you ride by in a taxi with a suitcase. So I knew you were in Berlin, and didn't know my address. I was terribly happy you'd arrived, but at the same time it was torture for me. I rushed over to the street where I used to live, and the concierge there told me you'd just stopped by and that he didn't know where to direct you. I've changed addresses so many times since. . . . It was all very stupid. Then I went home, forgot a package in the tram on the way, and began waiting. I knew you'd find me right away through Taubendorf. Still, it was very hard waiting. You only came after ten —

KUZNETSOFF

Listen, Olya —

OLGA PAVLOVNA

And left immediately. And you've only been to see me once since and then only for a moment.

KUZNETSOFF

Listen, Olya: when I decided it was best we didn't live together, you agreed with me, and said you weren't in love with me anymore either. But when you talk like you're talking now, I begin to think — no, let me finish — I begin to think you wouldn't mind reviving that love. It would bother me a lot if it turned out that, in spite of our decision, you still feel differently about me than I do about you.

OLGA PAVLOVNA

I can't talk about it today. Let's not. I thought I'd make you laugh with the story about the package.

KUZNETSOFF

No, I want to clear this up. . . .

OLGA PAVLOVNA

It's just that kind of day today. . . . Anyway, there are lots of things you are incapable of understanding. Imagine, say, the sound of a bad violin outside the window—just a moment ago, say, just before you came—actually it didn't happen, since even if I'd heard such a sound I wouldn't have cared. . . . Don't look at me that way. I'm telling you I wouldn't have cared. I don't love you. There was no violin.

KUZNETSOFF

I don't understand what you're talking about.

OLGA PAVLOVNA

No, you cannot understand.

KUZNETSOFF

(getting up)
You know, I'd better get going. . . .

OLGA PAVLOVNA

Two years ago, when we lived here in Berlin together, there was some silly, silly song, some dance tune, that boys whistled in the street and organ-grinders played. If you heard that song now you wouldn't even recognize it. . . .

KUZNETSOFF

This is very irritating.

OLGA PAVLOVNA

Stop it. I can't stand it when you get angry like that. Your eyes turn yellow. It's just that I'm nervous today. Don't. You . . . you're satisfied with your hotel?

KUZNETSOFF

You know, you ought to remarry.

OLGA PAVLOVNA

Sure, sure, I will. I'll do everything you want. Listen, would you like me to swear that I don't love you? I don't! Do you hear me?

KUZNETSOFF

Yes, I hear you. Still, I'm unhappy that we had to have this conversation. Right now I simply don't have the time to put my soul to work. And conversations like this put one's soul to work. I'll tell you something: I absolutely can't bear the idea of someone thinking about me with love, with longing, with concern. It distracts me.

OLGA PAVLOVNA

You're right, Alyosha, you're right. I don't want to distract you. There, it's all over. . . . In fact, there wasn't anything in the first place. You know, I have the feeling Taubendorf is courting me a little. *(laughs)* I like him a lot. I mean it, I really do.

KUZNETSOFF

I'm not quite satisfied with him. He's a little obtuse. With all his romanticism he lives in a dream world. Well, I must be off.

OLGA PAVLOVNA

Alyosha, do you ever think about what you . . . what they . . . well, about the danger?

KUZNETSOFF

Only my Aunt Nellie and the Man in the Moon think.

(walks toward the door)

OLGA PAVLOVNA
(calling after him)
Put on your coat. It's chilly out.
(After Kuznetsoff leaves, Olga Pavlovna remains standing by the table, running her finger along the pattern of the doily. Then she walks around the room: it is evident that she is holding back tears. Hearing footsteps outside the door, she sits down as before and picks up her embroidery. Without knocking, Marianna enters. She is very smartly dressed.)

MARIANNA
(breathlessly)
I ran into your husband outside. How old is he? *(glances fleetingly at the embroidery)* That certainly is pretty. How old is he?

OLGA PAVLOVNA
Thirty-two. Why do you ask?

MARIANNA
(takes off her coat and hat, and tosses her hair. She is blonde, with the aid of peroxide.)
I've never seen anything like it in my life. The traffic outside is atrocious, one car on top of the other, the policeman is performing all kinds of ballet gestures, the pedestrians are waiting for him to stop the traffic, and your husband, cool as a cucumber, goes and crosses! In a straight line. The cars honk at him, the policeman freezes in amazement in a Nizhinsky pose — no reaction, he goes straight across. And yet he looks so peaceable. . . . What's this part going to be — openwork or lace?

OLGA PAVLOVNA
Lace.

MARIANNA

I'm so happy there was no shooting today. I'm sick and tired of Moser. He just won't stop pestering me. Someone else might have taken advantage of it to make a career. But I can't. I don't know if you can understand what I mean, dear, but for me art is everything. Art is sacred. Somebody like Pia Mora, who sleeps around, can go for rides with Moser. But I can't. Nothing in life interests me except art. Nothing. How exhausted I get, though! I've got the most demanding part—the whole film hangs on me. I can imagine what bliss it will be to see it all on the screen afterwards. Good heavens, what's the matter with you, sweetie, what's wrong? Olga Pavlovna! Why are you crying? What happened, Olga Pavlovna?

OLGA PAVLOVNA

Don't pay any attention to me. . . . It's nothing. . . . It'll go away in a minute. . . .
(She cries, wiping her eyes with her fingers like a child.)

MARIANNA

What is it, what's the matter? Is something wrong? Come, tell me, sweetie.

OLGA PAVLOVNA

Give me a hankie.

MARIANNA

It's not quite clean. I'll get you another one.

OLGA PAVLOVNA

Never mind. . . . There, it's over. . . . I just didn't sleep well last night.

MARIANNA

You want me to run out and get some valerian drops? Oh, wait, I have some here.

OLGA PAVLOVNA

It's all right. Thanks, Marianna Sergeyevna. Really, it's all right. It's all over.

MARIANNA

Oh, you're crying again. What a shame. Here, drink this. Slowly. Now sit quietly. Let's chat about something.

OLGA PAVLOVNA

Let's chat about something. *(blows her nose and laughs)*

MARIANNA

Oh. I've been wanting to ask you for a long time. What exactly does Alexey Matveyevich do?

OLGA PAVLOVNA

I don't know exactly. (*laughs)* Your hankie is all soaked, look. He's involved in various commercial dealings.

MARIANNA

I hope you don't mind my asking—I believe that, in spite of everything, you're still friends—but there's something I did want to ask you. . . . He isn't a Bolshevik, is he?

OLGA PAVLOVNA

Do you hate Bolsheviks a lot, Marianna Sergeyevna?

MARIANNA

I despise them. Art is above politics. . . . But they debase art. They burn down marvelous Russian country houses.

Olga Pavlovna, don't tell me your husband . . .

OLGA PAVLOVNA
His personal life does not concern me. I don't want to know anything.

MARIANNA
(quickly)
And he never — never says anything to you?

OLGA PAVLOVNA
Never.

MARIANNA
Aha. *(short pause)* And I have very strong suspicions. Imagine, Oshivenski says he saw Alexey Matveyevich day before yesterday sitting in a café with a notorious agent from the Soviet Mission. Engaged in a very friendly conversation. Oshivenski and his wife are absolutely scandalized.

OLGA PAVLOVNA
I was just expecting them today. I don't particularly like that lady and I don't know why she keeps visiting me. But he's a sweet old man, and I'm very sorry for him.

MARIANNA
Still, it's an awful thing if it's true.

OLGA PAVLOVNA
I think your film is about Bolsheviks, isn't it?

MARIANNA
Oh, it's a wonderful film! Of course it's still too early to talk

about the plot because—you know—it's being shot in bits and pieces. I'm fully familiar only with my own part. But basically the screenplay has to do with the Russian Revolution. And of course there's a love story mixed in. Absolutely fascinating, I think, very *spannend.* The male lead is Harry Joy. He's a darling.
(a knock at the door. Kuznetsoff enters.)

KUZNETSOFF
You're still in this room, Olya. . . .

MARIANNA
Oh, Alexey Matveyevich, I'm glad to have her—

OLGA PAVLOVNA
You're back so soon!

KUZNETSOFF
Yes. *(to Marianna)* And you must teach me how to dance, Ma'am.

MARIANNA
May I? Want to try right now?

OLGA PAVLOVNA
(coming alive, with a radiant expression)
What is it, Alyosha? You seem so cheerful.

MARIANNA
I'll go ask the landlady for a phonograph. *(runs out)*

KUZNETSOFF
Olya, the deal went through. I'm getting even more than I expected. In ten days I'm going back.

OLGA PAVLOVNA
But you will be careful, won't you?

KUZNETSOFF
What does being careful have to do with it? I'm talking about money.

OLGA PAVLOVNA
I'm particularly afraid this time. But I'm glad for you. Really, I'm very glad.

KUZNETSOFF
Good.
(Marianna runs back in.)

MARIANNA
The landlady is grouchy today—she says the phonograph is broken.

OLGA PAVLOVNA
Oh, well, you'll do it another time.

MARIANNA
I told the maid to bring some coffee. She seems grouchy too.
(a knock at the door. Maid's voice: "Besuch für Frau Kuznetsoff.")

OLGA PAVLOVNA
Für mich? (goes out)

MARIANNA
Now, kiss me—quick!

KUZNETSOFF
No, no—please don't rush me, madam.

MARIANNA

Why "madam"? Why are you always so distant? When will you learn to be less formal with me? You don't want to kiss me? Alec!

KUZNETSOFF

Oh well, why not. . . .

MARIANNA

No, now I don't want to.

KUZNETSOFF

Oh, I keep forgetting to tell you—you shouldn't use any perfume at all.

MARIANNA

This is an excellent perfume. You don't understand a thing. It's Houbigant.

KUZNETSOFF
(sings half-voice)
And my beloved hooligan
gave me an ounce of Houbigant[4] . . .

MARIANNA

No, it was from a former admirer. Are you jealous?

KUZNETSOFF

Marianna, you want to know the truth?

MARIANNA

Yes, of course.

---

[4] The first syllable of Houbigant should be accented, and the name should be pronounced with an Anglo-American inflection.

KUZNETSOFF

All right—I'm not the least bit jealous. *(picks up the photograph and examines it again)* I've seen that face before.

MARIANNA

He was shot by the Bolsheviks last year. In Moscow. *(pause)* And why do you call me "madam"? It's getting unbearable! Alec, wake up!

KUZNETSOFF

(puts down the portrait, which he has been holding, lost in thought) Unbearable, is it? Less unbearable than "Alec."

MARIANNA

(perching on the arm of his chair and changing her tone of voice) You're an awfully strange man. I've never had such a strange love affair. I can't even understand how it happened. The way we met in the cellar. Then that crazy drunken evening with the Baron and Lyulya.... It's only been four days— yet it seems so long ago, doesn't it? I can't understand why I love you. . . . You're an ugly little thing. But I love you. You've got lots of charm. I love to kiss you here . . . and here....

KUZNETSOFF

You promised me some coffee.

MARIANNA

It's coming in a minute, my darling. Tell me, what if your wife—Oh yes!—tell me, you're not a Bolshevik, are you?

KUZNETSOFF

A Bolshevik, madam, a real Bolshevik.

MARIANNA

Cut it out—you keep kidding with me. It's strange. You don't appreciate one bit the fact that a refined woman like me got infatuated with you of all people. Don't start thinking it's love—it's only an infatuation. When I get tired of a lover I drop him like a wilted flower. But today you are mine, today you may love me. Why don't you say something?

KUZNETSOFF

Forgot my lines.

MARIANNA

You're absolutely impossible! You . . . you . . . I simply don't know what you are. You refuse to tell me anything about yourself. Wait, just a minute. . . . Darling. . . . Listen, Alec, why don't you want me to move into the hotel with you? That's the only place we meet anyway. Alec?

KUZNETSOFF

Listen, Marianna Sergeyevna, let's agree once and for all— no questions.

MARIANNA

All right, all right, I won't ask anything more. But I just don't understand. Why?
(voices outside the door. Then Olga Pavlovna brings in Yevghenia Vasilyevna Oshivenski, and Oshivenski himself follows. Yevghenia Vasilyevna is a plump old lady, dressed all in black, with slightly protruding eyes.)

OLGA PAVLOVNA

These people want to migrate over to your room, Marianna Sergeyevna.

OSHIVENSKI
We just wanted to peek in on you. Let's have your little hand.

MRS. OSHIVENSKI
That's a very becoming little dress, Mariánnochka.

MARIANNA
This is Olga Pavlovna's husband.

OSHIVENSKI
(dryly)
My pleasure.

MARIANNA
Oh, what am I saying. . . . I believe you already know each other. Sit down, dear Yevghenia Vasilyevna. Over here. Olga Pavlovna, you want to do the honors for me? I'm such a bad hostess. Please sit down, everybody.
(Meanwhile the maid has entered with a tray. On it are a coffeepot and cups. She sets it down, says "Bitte," and leaves.)

MRS. OSHIVENSKI
(to Marianna)
How are you, darling? Still making photographs?

OSHIVENSKI
Oh, Zhenya, you always mix things up! It's called shooting. Shooting a movie. . . .

MRS. OSHIVENSKI
I hear you play Communists in it?

MARIANNA
Please have some cake. Olga Pavlovna, would you cut

it? Yes, it's a very interesting film. Of course it's hard
to judge, because it's being shot—please have some—in bits
and pieces.

OSHIVENSKI

Thanks, I guess I will have a bitty piece. *(He glances at
Kuznetsoff, who has walked, with his cup, to the settee in the corner.)*
Why do they have to make movies about those scoundrels?

OLGA PAVLOVNA

Victor Ivanovich, how is your tavern doing?

OSHIVENSKI

And why are you changing the subject, Olga Pavlovna? I
repeat, these characters ought to be strangled, not trotted out
onto the stage.

MRS. OSHIVENSKI

I could strangle Trotsky with my own hands.

MARIANNA

Of course, art is above politics, but they have besmirched
everything—beauty, the poetry of life. . . .

MRS. OSHIVENSKI

I hear they have some great poet—Blok or Bloch[5]—or
whatever his name is. A Jew futurist. Well, they maintain
that this Bloch is better than Pushkin-and-Lermontov.
(She says it like "Laurel-and-Hardy.")

---

[5] The "ch" to be pronounced as "h."

OLGA PAVLOVNA

Come, come, Yevghenia Vasilyevna—Alexander Blok died a
long time ago. Besides—

MRS. OSHIVENSKI
(sailing on unperturbed)
But dearie, the whole point is that he's alive. They lie about it
deliberately. Just like they lied about Lenin. There were several Lenins. The real one was killed at the very beginning.

OSHIVENSKI
(continuing to glance to the left)
Those scoundrels are capable of anything. Excuse me. . . .
Olga Pavlovna, what's the name and patronymic of your—

KUZNETSOFF
Alexey Matveyich.[6] At your service.

OSHIVENSKI
I wanted to ask you, Alexey Matveyich—why are you
smiling like that?

KUZNETSOFF
To be polite. You keep looking over at me.

OSHIVENSKI
Emigré talk doesn't seem to be your cup of tea. Sir, you ought
to try—

OLGA PAVLOVNA
Can I give you some more coffee?

---

[6] A normal contraction of "Matveyevich" in spoken Russian.

OSHIVENSKI
—you ought to try living the way we live for a while. You'd start talking émigré talk yourself. Take me, for example. I'm an old man. They took away everything I had. They killed my son. For more than seven years I've been leading a pauper's existence in exile. And now I don't know what's going to happen next. Our way of thinking is very different from yours.

KUZNETSOFF
(laughing)
Why on earth are you attacking me like this?

MRS. OSHIVENSKI
Mariannochka, we must be going soon. *(in a rapid sotto voce)* Sorry, *mais je ne peux pas supporter la compagnie d'un bolchevik.*

OSHIVENSKI
No, I'm not attacking you. It's just hard to control oneself sometimes. The mood may be different in Warsaw. You were there, weren't you?

KUZNETSOFF
Passed through on my way. I've already answered that question for you.

OSHIVENSKI
And you're planning to stay here a long time?

KUZNETSOFF
No, I'm leaving soon.

OSHIVENSKI
And for where?

KUZNETSOFF
What do you mean where? The USSR, of course.
(silence)

MRS. OSHIVENSKI
Monsieur Kuznetsoff, perhaps you might be so kind as to take a little parcel with you? I have a granddaughter in St. Petersburg.

OSHIVENSKI
Zhenya!

KUZNETSOFF
If the parcel is not too big I'll take it.

OSHIVENSKI
And permit me to ask, how come they let you into Russia?

KUZNETSOFF
Why wouldn't they?

MARIANNA
Alexey Matveyevich, stop joking. God only knows what people will think.

KUZNETSOFF
If the interrogation is over, allow me to say good-by. Olya, I'd like to lie down for an hour in your room. I still have things to do tonight.

OLGA PAVLOVNA
Wait, I'll make you comfortable. . . .
(Olga Pavlovna and Kuznetsoff leave.)

OSHIVENSKI
How do you like that!

MRS. OSHIVENSKI
I had a feeling this would happen. Poor Olga Pavlovna. . . .
I'm beginning to understand a lot of things.

OSHIVENSKI
She's a fine one too. . . . If people decide to separate they
should stop seeing each other and acting like lovebirds! I'll
never shake his hand again, you have my word on that.

MARIANNA
Victor Ivanovich, I assure you—Alexey Matveyevich was
only joking. You got overly excited.

OSHIVENSKI
(gradually calming down)
No, I detest that kind of person. May I have some more
coffee!
(Marianna tilts the coffeepot.)

CURTAIN

ACT THREE

A very bare room: a vestibule, somewhat like an embryonic foyer. A slate-colored wall extends from the right along the proscenium, stops at center stage, and recedes, with the angle of its outline creating the proper perspective, into the distance, where one can see a door that leads into an auditorium. On the right, at the very edge of the stage, steps, with a copper handrail, lead down to the right. Against the wall, facing the audience, stands a small red velour settee. At the left edge, downstage, there is a table that serves as a box office, with a plain chair. Thus, someone who arrives for the lecture comes up the steps from the right, crosses from right to left along the slate wall enlivened by the red settee and either continues across the stage all the way to the left edge and the table where tickets are being sold, or else, having reached center stage, where the wall stops, turns, goes upstage and there disappears through the door leading into the hall. On the left wall there is a Toilette *sign and the red cone of a fire extinguisher above a folded hose. At the table sits Lyulya, a pert, attractive girl, with cosmetic footnotes, and beside her stands Taubendorf. Several people (typical émigrés) cross the stage, a bell rings, there is a confused sound of voices, and the stage grows empty. Everyone has gone through the upstage door. Only Lyulya and Taubendorf remain.*

LYULYA

Let's count how much we've taken in. Wait, let's do it this way —

TAUBENDORF

Not much, I think. Why is this money lying separately?

LYULYA

— eighteen — don't interrupt — eighteen-fifty, nineteen —

TAUBENDORF

Oh, how many times I've already done all this! . . . I'm lucky — as soon as they organize some lecture or concert or ball they always ask me to be in charge. I've even established a tariff: for a ball I get twenty-five.

LYULYA

There, I've lost count! Tsk-tsk. . . . Now I have to start all over again.

TAUBENDORF

Lectures, idiotic reports, charity balls, anniversaries — how many of them! Lyulya, I, too, have lost count. Now, for instance, someone is lecturing on something — but who it is and what, I really couldn't care less. Then again, maybe it's not a lecture at all but a concert, or else some long-haired moron reading poetry. Listen, Lyulya, let me count for you.

LYULYA

You say such strange things, Nikolay Karlovich. Today it should be especially interesting. And there are lots of people I know. This five is all torn.

TAUBENDORF

The faces are always the same. The same Professor

Vólkov, the Feldman girls, journalists, lawyers . . . all the faces are familiar. . . .

LYULYA
(powdering her face)
Well, if you'll really be a dear and count for me, I'll go inside—to me it's very interesting. May I powder your nose for you?

TAUBENDORF
Thanks a lot. By the way, don't forget—tomorrow is the last day of shooting. Go on, go on, I'll take care of everything here.

LYULYA
You are a sweetheart!
(Goes out through the upstage door. Taubendorf sits down at the table and counts the money. Olga Pavlovna, in coat and hat, enters from the right.)

OLGA PAVLOVNA
Is Alyosha here?

TAUBENDORF
You're the last person I expected! . . . No, I haven't seen him.

OLGA PAVLOVNA
That's odd.

TAUBENDORF
I'd never expect him to come to this kind of affair.

OLGA PAVLOVNA
There's a lecture of some kind going on here, isn't there? He told me Thursday that he planned to go.

TAUBENDORF

I really don't know. I ran into him on the street yesterday. He didn't say anything about it.

OLGA PAVLOVNA

That means I came for nothing.

TAUBENDORF

I wouldn't think émigré lectures could possibly interest him. Anyway, it only just started. He may still come.

OLGA PAVLOVNA

Could be. Let's sit down somewhere.
(They sit on the red settee.)

TAUBENDORF

I don't understand it—is it possible Alyosha hasn't been to see you in the last couple of days?

OLGA PAVLOVNA

The last time he came over was when the Oshivenskis were there—that would make it Thursday. And this is Sunday. I know he's very busy and so forth. But I have been feeling uneasy and very nervous these last days. Of course what worries me is not the fact that he doesn't come to see me but this business he's involved in. . . . Is everything going all right, Nikolay Karlovich?

TAUBENDORF

Splendidly. It sometimes almost makes my head spin when I think about the things that are happening.

OLGA PAVLOVNA

But the Communists are shrewd, they have spies and

agents provocateurs. . . . Alexey could get caught at any moment. . . .

TAUBENDORF
That's the whole point—they're not that shrewd.

OLGA PAVLOVNA
I wish I were living in the fifties of the last century, in the backwoods of Glúkhov or Mírgorod. I get so scared and so sad.

TAUBENDORF
Olga Pavlovna, you remember our last conversation?

OLGA PAVLOVNA
Which one? Before Alexey's arrival?

TAUBENDORF
Yes. I told you—you may recall—that when you feel sad and scared—as you just put it—I told you that then—that in moments like this, I'm ready—what I mean is, I'm ready to do anything for you.

OLGA PAVLOVNA
I remember. Thank you, my dear. Only—

TAUBENDORF
(getting up and pacing about the stage)
There's nothing I wouldn't . . . I've already known you for three years. I was best man at your wedding—remember?— at that little church in Tegel.[7] Then, when you separated,

---

[7] A suburb of Berlin where there were (and are) a Russian church and cemetery.

when you fell out of love with your husband—and remained alone—already then there was a lot I wanted to say to you. But I have a strong will. I decided not to rush things. Three times Alyosha traveled to Russia, and I would come to see you—but not too often, right? It was deliberate. I had a feeling there might be . . . well, all kinds of things— maybe you were seeing someone else . . . and maybe it wasn't fair to Alyosha . . . it just didn't seem right. But now I realize. . . .

OLGA PAVLOVNA

Nikolay Karlovich, for heaven's sake, don't. . . .

TAUBENDORF

Now I realize that I need wait no longer—I realize that you and Alyosha are like total strangers. He wouldn't be able to understand you anyway. I don't blame him for it—you see, I have no right to criticize him or even discuss his actions. He is magnificent, he is something very special. . . . But—he has given you up for Russia. He is simply incapable of other interests. That's why I don't feel any guilt toward him.

OLGA PAVLOVNA

I don't know if you should be telling me all this, Nikolay Karlovich.

TAUBENDORF

(sitting down again)

Of course I should. It's practically impossible to keep silent. Listen: I ask nothing of you. I mean, that's nonsense—of course I ask, and I ask a great deal. Maybe if one tries, if one makes a real effort, one can force oneself—well, at least to notice a person.

OLGA PAVLOVNA

Wait. . . . There's a misunderstanding here.

TAUBENDORF

No, no! I know everything you're going to say. I know that for you I am nothing more than Nikolay Karlovich, and that's the end of it. But then, you don't notice anybody. For you, too, the only thing in life is your longing for Russia. And I can't live like that. . . . For you I would give up everything. . . . God knows I'd like to get back over there too, but for you I'd stay, for you I'd do anything. . . .

OLGA PAVLOVNA

Please wait a minute. Calm down. Give me your hand. Please calm down. Your forehead is even perspiring. I want to tell you something very different.

TAUBENDORF

But why? Why? You would never feel sad with me. You're only sad because you're alone. I would surround you . . . you're my joy. . . .

OLGA PAVLOVNA

I'll tell you something I've never told anybody before. You see, you . . . you are mistaken. I'll tell you the truth. I'm not interested in Russia now — I mean, I'm interested, but not all that passionately. The point is I've never stopped loving my husband. *(silence)*

TAUBENDORF

Oh. Yes, that changes everything.

OLGA PAVLOVNA

No one knows this. Even he doesn't know.

TAUBENDORF
Yes, of course.

OLGA PAVLOVNA
To me he is not at all a leader and a hero as he is for you—but simply . . . I simply love him, his way of speaking, walking, raising his eyebrows when he finds something funny. Sometimes I feel I'd like to arrange for him to be caught and put in jail forever, and for me to be in that jail with him.

TAUBENDORF
He'd escape.

OLGA PAVLOVNA
Now you want to hurt me. Yes, he'd escape. That's exactly my misfortune. But there's nothing I can do to change it.

TAUBENDORF
Thirteen.

OLGA PAVLOVNA
Pardon me?

TAUBENDORF
I was just counting the money, and when you came in I stopped at thirteen. Unlucky number.
(silence)

OLGA PAVLOVNA
Does it add up to much?

TAUBENDORF
No, not much I think. Just barely enough to pay for the

hall. What difference does it make?

OLGA PAVLOVNA
Nikolay Karlovich, you understand, of course, that Alyosha must not find out about what I told you. Don't talk to him about me.

TAUBENDORF
I understand everything, Olga Pavlovna.

OLGA PAVLOVNA
I guess he isn't coming.
(They both get up.)

TAUBENDORF
He and I have an appointment to meet tomorrow morning at the studio. It's an awfully silly place for a business meeting, but there was no other way. Would you like me to give him any kind of message at all?

OLGA PAVLOVNA
No, nothing. I'm sure he'll drop by to see me tomorrow anyway. And now I'll run along.

TAUBENDORF
Please excuse me for . . . for what I said. I had no way of knowing.

OLGA PAVLOVNA
Of course. Probably it's my own fault. Well, so long.

TAUBENDORF
Olga Pavlovna, you have my admiration. You are an absolutely marvelous person. Alyosha does not understand.

OLGA PAVLOVNA

Oh, Nikolay Karlovich, really—let's not talk about it any more. . . . After all, I'm not the Chinese language that one either understands or doesn't understand. Believe me, there is nothing incomprehensible about me.

TAUBENDORF

I didn't want to make you angry.

OLGA PAVLOVNA

Well, some time I'll get truly rebellious, then we'll see. . . . *(laughs)* The sparks will really fly! . . .
(She leaves. Taubendorf returns to the table and sits down. In the hall, on the other side of the wall, there is a thunder of applause.)

CURTAIN

ACT FOUR

The lobby of a film studio. On the right, along the edge of the stage, the same gray wall as in the preceding act. To the left of it, a wide passageway crowded with movie props, creating an effect reminiscent simultaneously of a photographer's waiting room, the jumble of an amusement-park booth, and the motley corner of a futurist's canvas. (Among these angular shapes are conspicuous three cupolas — a large one and two smaller ones — the ochre, onion-shaped domes of some crudely reproduced Russian church. There is also a balalaika lying here haphazardly, and a half-unfurled map of Russia.) These props have uneven gaps and apertures (in the distance are visible the outlines of enormous klieg lights). All of it reminds the viewer of a many-colored jigsaw puzzle, carelessly and only partially assembled. As the curtain rises, the front of the stage is swarming with Russian émigrés who have just arrived for the shooting. Among them is Lyulya. The Assistant Director briskly and buoyantly squeezes onstage through the scenery blocking his way. He is redheaded, has a paunch, wears neither jacket nor waistcoat, and immediately begins to speak very loudly.

ASSISTANT DIRECTOR
Get your makeup on, people, get your makeup on!

Ladies to the left, men to the right. How come Marianna isn't here yet? The call was for nine o'clock. . . .
(The stage empties. Then two stagehands in blue carry a ladder across.)

ASSISTANT DIRECTOR'S VOICE
(already backstage)
Kurt, Kurt! Wo ist Kurt? Mann muss —
(The voice fades away. Then Marianna and Kuznetsoff enter from the right.)

MARIANNA
(pressing her hands to her temples as she walks)
It's absolutely outrageous, absolutely outrageous of you. . . .

KUZNETSOFF
. . . only one thing can be interesting in life—that which can be prevented. Why waste energy worrying about the inevitable?
(They both stop.)

MARIANNA
So you haven't changed your mind?

KUZNETSOFF
(looking around)
Amusing place. . . . I've never been in a film studio before. *(peeking behind the props)* Look at those gigantic lamps! . . .

MARIANNA
I probably won't understand you until my dying day. So your decision is final?

ASSISTANT DIRECTOR
(running in from the right)
What's going on here, Mariannochka? This simply won't
do.... Shoo! Into your dressing room!

MARIANNA
All right, all right, in a minute.

ASSISTANT DIRECTOR
Not in a minute, but immediately. Kurt! *(runs off)*

MARIANNA
Think it over again. . . . Think it over while I'm changing.
Understand?

KUZNETSOFF
Ah, Marianna Sergeyevna, you're really so . . .

MARIANNA
No, no. Just wait for me here and think it over.
(Exits to the right. Assistant Director runs in from left.)

ASSISTANT DIRECTOR
Please go get made up. Didn't you hear me?

KUZNETSOFF
Relax. I don't work here.

ASSISTANT DIRECTOR
Then you're not supposed to be here. There are rules.

KUZNETSOFF
Fiddlesticks.

ASSISTANT DIRECTOR
If Herr Moser—

KUZNETSOFF
Childhood friend of mine.

ASSISTANT DIRECTOR
Oh, in that case it's all right. Excuse me.

KUZNETSOFF
You people pour on the folklore pretty thick. What are those, cupolas?

ASSISTANT DIRECTOR
Yes. Today is the last day of shooting—the uprising scene. We're in a terrible rush, since the film has to be all edited by Saturday. *Pardon,* I have to run. *(runs off)*

KUZNETSOFF
Go right ahead.
(Walks to and fro, picks up and unfurls the enormous map crudely depicting Russia. Smiles and examines it. Taubendorf comes in from the right. Beneath his coat are visible jackboots. He is carrying a valise.)

TAUBENDORF
Oh, you're already here, Alyosha. How did you get in?

KUZNETSOFF
Very simple. Said I was the bosom buddy of somebody called Moser. The Crimea came out as a perfect rhomboid here.

TAUBENDORF
Russia. . . . Yes. My colleagues are probably already getting made up. But that's all right. Everything goes at a

snail's pace here. . . . Alyosha, I carried out all your orders.
Werner is already on his way.

KUZNETSOFF

Jesus, it's dusty in here.
*(Tosses the map into a corner. It rolls up by itself. Claps his hands to
get the dust off them.)*

TAUBENDORF

Alyosha, when will you arrange a passport for me too?

KUZNETSOFF

Later. Here's why I wanted to see you: Saturday I'm
going back to Russia; in about three weeks Démidov will get
here. I'll ask you to. . . . This isn't a very good place to talk,
though.

TAUBENDORF

Let's go over there—there's an empty room in back. In the
meantime I can get my makeup on.

KUZNETSOFF

Aha! You're in jackboots. . . .
*(Both exeunt left. Assistant Director scurries across the stage and
darts behind the scenery. Stagehands pass carrying painted flats.
Made-up extras, the men in Russian shirts and the women in
kerchiefs, enter from right and left and gradually disappear behind
the scenery. Assistant Director runs out again, holding a huge
megaphone.)*

ASSISTANT DIRECTOR

Hurry up, people, hurry up! Everybody on the set!
We're starting as soon as Harry and Marianna are ready.

LYULYA
(with a kerchief on her head)
Harry's been ready for a long time. He's drinking beer in the canteen. *(leaves with the others)*

ASSISTANT DIRECTOR
(to Marianna)
Finally!...

MARIANNA
Did you see where. . . . There was a gentleman here. . . . The one I came with. . . .

ASSISTANT DIRECTOR
What's the matter with you? We're here for serious work, not tomfoolery. On the set please!
(He runs off. Kuznetsoff enters from the left.)

MARIANNA
Alec, it's such a madhouse here. . . . We'll never settle anything. Alec, have you changed your mind?

KUZNETSOFF
I didn't recognize you right away. Look at you, all yellow and purple.

MARIANNA
I'm supposed to look like this. It comes out quite differently on the screen. . . . Alec!

KUZNETSOFF
And that astrakhan hat with the star on it. Who are you supposed to be?

MARIANNA
You're driving me insane!
(Assistant Director runs in.)

ASSISTANT DIRECTOR
We're starting! Let's go, for God's sake! The rushes have to be ready by Saturday. Marianna! *(yells right at her through the megaphone)* Places!!

MARIANNA
You're abominably rude. Alec, I implore you, wait for me.... I'll only be a minute....
(Marianna and Assistant Director leave. From the left appears Taubendorf with a false beard and a Russian peasant shirt and cap.)

TAUBENDORF
There. I'm ready too.

KUZNETSOFF
Lovely, lovely. I think they've already started in there. Your commander is very excited.

TAUBENDORF
That's normal. First there'll be endless rehearsals of this uprising scene. The actual shooting will start much later. *(lights a cigarette)* Alyosha, have we covered everything? There's nothing else?
(As he speaks, he leans against a wall on which there is a large "nicht rauchen" sign. He continues to smoke.)

KUZNETSOFF
Nothing else. The rest you know yourself.

TAUBENDORF
The rest?

KUZNETSOFF
Yes. About Olga Pavlovna. Take care of her as you did before. Look in on her now and then, and help her out if necessary.

TAUBENDORF
Alyosha, I . . .

KUZNETSOFF
What's the matter with you?

TAUBENDORF
(very agitated)
Actually . . .

KUZNETSOFF
Shoot.

TAUBENDORF
Alyosha, I beg you. . . . I want to go with you! Do you hear, I want to go with you! To stay here will be my undoing. . . .
(From backstage comes the buzzing of klieg lights, then the Assistant Director's voice through the megaphone.)

MEGAPHONE BACKSTAGE
People, you're in Russia! In a square! There's an uprising going on! First Group waves their flags! Second Group runs left from the barricade! Third Group moves forward!

KUZNETSOFF
You're beginning to bore me, my friend. I've already told you everything.

TAUBENDORF

I dare not contradict you. What—are you going now?
Will I see you again?

MEGAPHONE BACKSTAGE

Achtung!

KUZNETSOFF

No, I don't think so. I won't have much free time these
last few days. I'll drop in on Olga Pavlovna for a minute
today, and then not until Saturday, before leaving. There's
something else I wanted to ask you: are you going to keep
working in the tavern?

TAUBENDORF

No, no—it's closing tomorrow. And this is the last day
of shooting, too. I'll find something or other.

KUZNETSOFF

Well, there's shooting and shooting. Let's say good-by.
(They embrace.)

TAUBENDORF

God bless you. . . .
*(When Taubendorf goes through the door Kuznetsoff whips out a
Browning and aims at him.)*

KUZNETSOFF

Hold it!

TAUBENDORF

Alyosha, someone might see you. *(leaves)*

KUZNETSOFF

Good for him. . . . Didn't even flinch. . . . And you, my

friend, don't you let me down. *(addressing the pistol, which he aims at the audience)* Don't you flinch in the clinch. *(puts it back in his pocket)*
(A stagehand runs in and carries off the map and the balalaika. Kuznetsoff consults his watch. Buzzing of the klieg lights offstage. Marianna hurries in. She sheds her fur hat and gives her hair a toss.)

KUZNETSOFF
Marianna Sergeyevna, I'm afraid I have to be going.

MARIANNA
Alec!

KUZNETSOFF
You've done your part already?

MARIANNA
No, no. . . . I'll only be starting in a minute. I have a scene with the male lead. But that's not the point. Alec, are you still planning to leave on Saturday?

KUZNETSOFF
Yes.

MARIANNA
I can't believe this. I can't believe you are leaving me. Listen, Alec, listen. . . . I'll give up the stage. I'll forget about my talent. I'll go with you. Take me away somewhere. We'll live somewhere in the South, in Nice. . . . Your silly commercial dealings can wait. Something horrible is happening to me. I've already ordered dresses, bright, wonderful dresses for the South. . . . I thought. . . . No, tell

me you're not going off and leaving me! I'll caress you. You know how good I am at it, don't you? We'll have a villa full of flowers. We'll be so happy. . . . You'll see. . . .

MEGAPHONE BACKSTAGE

Everybody back! Everybody back! It isn't worth a damn! Listen, when I say "One!"—that's when Group One gets up. And when I say "Two!" Group Two runs left. Quiet! *Achtung!*

KUZNETSOFF

I had a good time with you. But now I'm leaving.

MARIANNA

Alec, what is the meaning of this?

MEGAPHONE BACKSTAGE

One!

KUZNETSOFF

I don't think I ever gave you reason to believe that our relationship would last. I am a very busy man. To tell you the truth, I don't even have the time to say I am a busy man.

MARIANNA

Oh, so that's the way it is. . . . Then let me tell you something too. It was all playacting. I was just doing a part. I feel nothing but revulsion for you. I'm the one who's leaving you, not the other way around. And one other thing—I know you're a Bolshevik, a KGB agent, God knows what else. . . . You disgust me!

MEGAPHONE BACKSTAGE

Two!

MARIANNA

You're a Bolshevik! Get out of here. Don't you dare come back to me. Don't you dare write me. No, it doesn't matter— I know you'll write anyway, but I'll tear up your letters.

MEGAPHONE BACKSTAGE

Three!

KUZNETSOFF

No, no, Marianna Sergeyevna, I have no intention of writing. Anyway, right now you're only making me late. It's time for me to go.

MARIANNA

Do you realize that you'll never see me again?

KUZNETSOFF

Yes, of course—what's the point of repeating yourself all the time? Say good-by.

MARIANNA

(turning away)
No.
(Kuznetsoff bows and unhurriedly goes off right. Stagehands walk toward him carrying banners, and a bundle of rifles. He slows, glancing at them with a fleeting smile, then leaves. Marianna is left standing by the scenery at the left.)

MEGAPHONE BACKSTAGE

Back! Everybody back! It's no good! People, I'm telling you for the last time—listen . . . Group One—

CURTAIN

ACT FIVE

The Oshivenskis' room. On the left, a door to the entrance hall; in the rear wall, a smaller door to the adjoining room; on the right, a window onto the courtyard. Against the rear wall, to the left of the door, the bare metal frame of a double bed, its springs exposed; next to it a night table (propped against the wall, evidently because one leg has broken off) with its door wide open; by the bed a small rug lies askew, with one corner folded back. To the right of the door, several suitcases (one of them is open), a Russian wooden trunk with hasps, a hamper, a carton with a squashed top, and a large bundle. The floor around the suitcases is mottled with scraps of white and brown paper; the bare table has been moved over to the window, while the wastebasket remains where the table used to stand in the middle of the room and, lying on its side, disgorges various trash. The chairs stand helter-skelter; one of them has been moved up against the wardrobe (which is by the rear wall, to the right of the door), from whose top things have apparently been removed since a whole newspaper page hangs down on one side. The walls of the room are covered with suspicious water stains; and a monstrous chandelier, suspended from the ceiling (Bavarian workmanship: a Gretchen with a dolphin's tale from which extend, curving upward, deer antlers crowned with light bulbs), gazes reproachfully at the dust, at the absurd placement of the chairs, at the baggage of the departing tenants.

OSHIVENSKI
(as he finishes packing a suitcase)
Junk. . . .

MRS. OSHIVENSKI
Another piece of string would be handy. . . .

OSHIVENSKI
There is no more string. Junk.

MRS. OSHIVENSKI
And where are we supposed to go now? Oh my dear God. . . .

OSHIVENSKI
We'll move straight into the Kingdom of Heaven. At least there you don't have to pay the rent in advance.

MRS. OSHIVENSKI
Shame on you, Vitya, for talking like that. A crying shame. Here, help me lock this trunk.

OSHIVENSKI
What a miserable life. . . . No—I've had enough!

MRS. OSHIVENSKI
Just be careful, Vitya . . . when you start talking with him. . . . We can put the trunk over against the wall for now.

OSHIVENSKI
Against the wall. . . . Against the wall. . . . Enough is

enough. We've done our share of suffering. Anything would be better. Even the wall and the firing squad.

MRS. OSHIVENSKI

You stick mostly to questions—you know, what and where. . . .

OSHIVENSKI

Even one's honor goes to the dogs. That's enough. What are you bawling about?

MRS. OSHIVENSKI

You won't find Vasya's grave anyway. There is no grave. Even if you search all of Russia. . . .

OSHIVENSKI

You'd better get the parcel ready. Damn these newspapers—they keep rustling under one's feet. . . . I'll start bawling myself in a minute. Stop it, Zhenya. . . .

MRS. OSHIVENSKI

I don't trust him. A man like that might filch it.

OSHIVENSKI
(sitting down at the table)
Stop the nonsense—that's got nothing to do with it. And why on earth are you sending that *halva?*

MRS. OSHIVENSKI

Oh, the *halva* is unimportant. The main thing is that he get the fabric to them. . . .

OSHIVENSKI

And where do we get the money to settle with the

landlady—answer that one! *(At the word "money" he hits the table violently with the palm of his hand.)* I can just hear her screeching like a parrot. . . .

MRS. OSHIVENSKI
If I had another piece of string. . . .
(A knock at the door; Marianna enters. She is wearing a sober dark suit, as if she were in mourning.)

OSHIVENSKI
(without enthusiasm)
Welcome. . . .

MARIANNA
Excuse me. . . . You're packing. . . . I'm disturbing you. . . .

MRS. OSHIVENSKI
Come on in, honey. It's all right, we're finished.

MARIANNA
Yes. . . . If I may. . . .

OSHIVENSKI
My little tavern—remember? Eh? Nice little tavern, wasn't it, eh? The passing legs, eh? Look at us now. Nothing but a fourth-class ticket to join our ancestors.

MRS. OSHIVENSKI
You're so pale! Honey, what's the matter? You look like a ghost.

MARIANNA
Oh, please don't look at me like that. Please don't.

OSHIVENSKI
(getting up)
Well, Zhenya, wish me luck. I'm off to confabulate with the landlady. Perhaps she'll take pity on us.

MRS. OSHIVENSKI
Go ahead, go ahead. Marianna and I will stay here and have a cup of tea. Oh, I forgot—all the china is packed. Forgive me.
(Oshivenski has left.)

MARIANNA
Yevghenia Vasilyevna, I've had a catastrophe.

MRS. OSHIVENSKI
I can see, I can see, dear—you're so listless, so quiet, that I hardly recognize you.

MARIANNA
A terrible catastrophe. I just saw the first screening.

MRS. OSHIVENSKI
What screening was that, dear?

MARIANNA
Oh, you know—I had a part in a film. And yesterday the picture was screened for the first time.

MRS. OSHIVENSKI
Then what was the catastrophe? A fire, or what?

MARIANNA
Yes, a fire. Everything I had has been destroyed—my dreams, my faith in myself, my life. I'm totally ruined.

MRS. OSHIVENSKI

Oh, yes, by the way — there was a favor I wanted to ask you, darling. But we can talk about it later. Tell me what happened.

MARIANNA

I saw myself on the screen. It was monstrous. I had waited with such anticipation for the moment when I would see myself, and finally that moment came. An absolute horror. In one place, for instance, I'm lying flat on the couch and then I get up. When we were shooting, I thought I was so graceful, so vivacious. But when I saw myself on the screen, Yevghenia Vasilyevna, I got up—excuse the expression— bottom first. . . . I stuck out my behind and made such a clumsy turn! And it was like that all the way through. Artificial, horrendous gestures. And here that lousy Pia Mora glides around like a swan. It's mortifying. . . .

MRS. OSHIVENSKI

It's not as bad as all that, darling. You should see how I came out on my passport photo. A mug you wouldn't believe.

MARIANNA

And that's only the beginning: this was just a private screening for us. But now the film is going to be shown all over Berlin, and then all over the world, and with it my ridiculous gestures and grimaces, my unbelievable gait. . . .

MRS. OSHIVENSKI

Here's what I wanted to ask you, my dear. We have to move and we don't have a penny. Do you think you might be able to make us a loan of fifty marks or so?

MARIANNA

A loan? Oh, so that's what you were talking about. . . . I

guess I'm walking around in a kind of fog today. No, Yevghenia Vasilyevna, I'm broke too. I spent all my earnings on dresses.

MRS. OSHIVENSKI

Shame on you, you clotheshorse. Well, I guess that's that. . . .

MARIANNA

On dresses! I bought myself a beautiful, white, Paris original. And you know for what? So I could. . . . Oh, there's no use talking about it! . . .

MRS. OSHIVENSKI

Tell me, tell me—you know, I wouldn't breathe a word, I never gossip.

MARIANNA

I couldn't care less about the film. That's not it at all. The point is that I fell in love, fell in love like an idiot. Got hooked, in other words. And he left me. That's all there is to it.

MRS. OSHIVENSKI

Who was it? Some German?

MARIANNA

He could have been a German or a Chinaman—what difference does it make? . . . Or an American.

MRS. OSHIVENSKI

Time heals all wounds, dear. Things aren't easy for any of us. Little Mara, your namesake and my granddaughter, was also abandoned by her husband. All because they got married in a civil ceremony. Yes, life isn't easy. What will become of my old Vitya and me now? Where do we go? I have absolutely no idea.

MARIANNA
Yevghenia Vasilyevna, may I make a phone call?

MRS. OSHIVENSKI
Go into that room over there. The tenant left but the telephone is still connected. Don't worry, there's no one there.
(Marianna leaves by the door in the rear wall. Grunting and holding up the hem of her skirt, Mrs. Oshivenski shoves a suitcase into a corner with her foot. She bends over and checks the lock. There is a knock at the door.)

MRS. OSHIVENSKI
Come in. *Herein.*
(Kuznetsoff hurries in.)

KUZNETSOFF
Quite a mess you have here.

MRS. OSHIVENSKI
Oh, thanks for dropping by. . . . Very kind of you. . . .

KUZNETSOFF
My wife gave me your message. I came for the parcel.

MRS. OSHIVENSKI
Yes, yes, of course. . . . Thank you so much.

KUZNETSOFF
I'm in a hurry.

MRS. OSHIVENSKI

Oh, but my husband wanted to have a chat with you. It was about something very important.

KUZNETSOFF

My train leaves at seven. I have to make one more stop before my departure.

MRS. OSHIVENSKI

My husband is downstairs—he'll be here in a minute. Couldn't you just wait for him, my dear sir?

KUZNETSOFF

I can't right now. By the way, your parcel is pretty hefty. If you wish I can look in again on my way to the station.

MRS. OSHIVENSKI

Oh, that would be so nice! Here's the address—is it clear?

KUZNETSOFF

Yes, certainly. Only now it's not Morskáya Street but Herzen Street.

MRS. OSHIVENSKI

What do we know: Herzen, Trotsky—who can tell them apart. . . . Don't lose the parcel. Regards to dear Olga Pavlovna.

KUZNETSOFF

No—I've already said good-by to her. So long. I'll drop by in half an hour. *(leaves)*
(Marianna returns, listlessly crosses the room, listlessly sinks into a chair.)

MARIANNA
He's gone.

MRS. OSHIVENSKI
You mean Kolya, dear?

MARIANNA
(angrily)
And good riddance! It's best that way.

MRS. OSHIVENSKI
The world is full of ways. In my time there was only one—straight and simple, while nowadays there is any number of them—twisted ones, crooked ones. We're being buffeted right and left. And you want me to tell you where it all comes from, what the root of the evil is—
(Oshivenski enters.)

OSHIVENSKI
No luck. She started talking about the police. *(sits down and drums on the table)*

MRS. OSHIVENSKI
What will become of us now? Oh my Lord. . . .

OSHIVENSKI
Just don't you start whimpering.

MARIANNA
I'll be running along.

MRS. OSHIVENSKI
You do look dejected today, dear. Well, go on and God bless you. Things aren't very joyful here either.

OSHIVENSKI

Good-by and good luck. We'll meet in Paradise, God willing.

MARIANNA
(apathetically)
Yes, yes, we'll phone each other some time. *(leaves)*

OSHIVENSKI
Floozie!

MRS. OSHIVENSKI

Vitya, I didn't want to say it in front of her, or else all of Berlin would find out that our house is frequented by Bolsheviks. *He* came for the parcel.

OSHIVENSKI

Why didn't you ask him to wait? You're really something!

MRS. OSHIVENSKI

Just a minute. . . . He promised to stop by again before he leaves. *(knock at the door)* Come in. *Herein.*
(Fyodor Fyodorovich enters; he is wearing a khaki suit with a belted jacket, and carries a walking stick.)

FYODOR FYODOROVICH

I ran into Marianna Sergeyevna right outside your building and, can you imagine, she didn't recognize me. Downright amazing!

MRS. OSHIVENSKI

Well, what's new, Fyodor Fyodorovich? Did you find something?

FYODOR FYODOROVICH

I did. Five Paradise Street, care of Engel; courtyard entrance, fifth floor. Unprepossessing but extremely cheap room.

MRS. OSHIVENSKI

How much is it?

FYODOR FYODOROVICH

Twenty-five. Including gas lighting and use of kitchen.

OSHIVENSKI

This is all idle talk. . . . We can't move out of here without paying anyway. And not a pfennig to our name.

FYODOR FYODOROVICH

Now don't you worry, Victor Ivanovich. It's true I don't have any money either, but I think I can come up with some by tomorrow.

OSHIVENSKI

We've got to move out today. *(strikes the table)* Anyway, that's beside the point. If we don't croak here, we'll croak there. . . .

MRS. OSHIVENSKI

Oh, Vitya, stop saying such horrid things. Fyodor Fyodorovich, did you say use of the kitchen was included?

FYODOR FYODOROVICH

Absolutely. Want to go have a look at it right now?

MRS. OSHIVENSKI

Yes — let's, dear. Why waste time?

FYODOR FYODOROVICH

As for me, I'm in a really jolly mood today. A pal of mine in Paris bought four taxicabs and is hiring me as a driver. He's even sending money for my ticket. I'm already working on my visa.

OSHIVENSKI

(through clenched teeth, shaking his head in time to the words)

Oh, isn't life wonderful!

FYODOR FYODOROVICH

Of course it's wonderful. I like variety. I'm grateful to Communism — it made us discover the whole wide world. Now I'm going to see Paris — new city, new impressions, the Eiffel Tower. It's a great feeling....

MRS. OSHIVENSKI

All right, I'm ready. Let's go.

OSHIVENSKI

(to Fyodor Fyodorovich)

You and your Eiffel Tower.... Oh, well....

FYODOR FYODOROVICH

Now don't you worry, Victor Ivanovich. Everything will be fine. You'll see. The room is clean, I'd even say very clean.

MRS. OSHIVENSKI

Come, dear, hurry up.

FYODOR FYODOROVICH

Bye-bye, Victor Ivanovich.

(Fyodor Fyodorovich and Mrs. Oshivenski leave. Oshivenski sits motionless for some time, hunched over and with the fingers of his hand, numbed by the drumming, outspread on the edge of the table. Then, outside the window, the squeaky, cracking strains of a very poorly played violin become audible. It is the same melody that Olga Pavlovna heard at the opening of Act II.)

OSHIVENSKI

Oh, that damn music! I'd like to take those catgut scrapers and . . .
(With a loud banging Kuznetsoff hurries in, carrying a suitcase. He, too, hears the violin and, while setting down the suitcase, holds it for a second in midair. The music breaks off.)

KUZNETSOFF

That's amusing—I know that tune. *(sits down)* So. At your service.

OSHIVENSKI

You see me in a moment of dire distress. I wanted to ask for your help.

KUZNETSOFF

I heard your little tavern folded, isn't that so?

OSHIVENSKI

That's the whole point. I invested every last penny in it. Everything went down the drain.

KUZNETSOFF

Is this furniture yours?

OSHIVENSKI

No. It came with the room. I don't have anything of my own.

KUZNETSOFF

So what do you plan to do now?

OSHIVENSKI

That's the problem. Do you think you might be able to give me some kind of advice? I'd really like to have some advice from you.

KUZNETSOFF

You want something practical, something specific?

OSHIVENSKI

Here's what I want to ask you: do you think that perhaps the concept itself contains some kind of hidden flaw?

KUZNETSOFF

Come on, come to the point. What concept?

OSHIVENSKI

Okay. If you insist that I spell things out for you, I'll be explicit. Say I—Mr. Ivánov, together with Mr. Petróv and Mr. Semyónov, decided, a few years ago, to winter at the Devil's quarters—in other words, to become émigrés, God willing. Now I ask you: do you find this wise, necessary, expedient? Or is the very concept silly?

KUZNETSOFF

Oh, I see. What you're trying to say is that you're fed up with being an émigré.

OSHIVENSKI

I'm fed up with the accursed existence I've been leading here. I'm fed up with perpetual indigence, Berlin back alleys, the repulsive rasp of a foreign tongue, this furniture, these newspapers, all these trashy trappings of émigré life. I am a former landowner. I was ruined right at the start. But I want you to understand: I don't need my land back. I need the Russian land. And if I were given the chance to set foot on it for no other reason than to dig my own grave, I would accept.

KUZNETSOFF

Let's put it all simply, without metaphors. So you'd like to come to the USSR, that is, to Russia?

OSHIVENSKI

I know you are a Communist—that's why I can be candid with you. I renounce the émigré pipe dream. I recognize the Soviet Government. I ask you to intercede on my behalf.

KUZNETSOFF

Are you being serious?

OSHIVENSKI

I have no intention of joking at a time like this. I have the feeling that with your protection they would pardon me, give me a passport, let me into Russia.

KUZNETSOFF

First of all, get out of the habit of saying "Russia." The country has a different name now. Secondly, I must inform you of the following: people like you do not get pardoned by the Soviet Government. I can perfectly well believe that you have a desire to go home. But everything else you say is claptrap. You reek of the old regime from over a thousand miles away. It may not be your fault, but it's so.

OSHIVENSKI

Hey, just a minute! How dare you use that tone with me? What do you think you're going to do, lecture me?

KUZNETSOFF

I am fulfilling your request. You wanted my opinion, didn't you?

OSHIVENSKI

What do I care about your opinion. I'm so homesick I could die, and you talk to me of old regimes. All right, I'll be frank with you. I decided in my old age to do a little boot-licking, and I don't know how to do it, I simply don't. I'm dying to see Russia, it's true. But to prostrate myself before the Soviets . . . no, my friend, you've got the wrong person. If you allow me, I'll be glad to fill out an application . . . and I'll go—but once I'm there I'll go to your phony heroes and spit in their faces, in the faces of all that thieving riffraff.

KUZNETSOFF
(consulting his watch)
Well, now at least you're being sincere. Can I consider our conversation terminated?

OSHIVENSKI

Oh, there's lots more I'd like to say to you. But you're in my home and I wouldn't feel right about it. . . .

KUZNETSOFF
Now may I take leave of you?
(Olga Pavlovna enters without knocking.)

KUZNETSOFF
I didn't think I'd see you again before leaving.

OSHIVENSKI

What's the matter, Olga Pavlovna, why are you standing there like a statue? Come in, come in. . . .

OLGA PAVLOVNA

No, Alyosha, I didn't either. *(to Oshivenski)* Actually, I dropped by because not long ago I had a call from Marianna, who happened to mention that you were planning to move—Oh, you have your suitcase here too—And . . . oh, yes. . . I thought it must be very hard for you, with no money and all. . . .

OSHIVENSKI

No, it's all right. We'll dig some up somewhere. It doesn't matter much.

OLGA PAVLOVNA

Nevertheless . . . I do have a little extra cash.

OSHIVENSKI

Oh well, if that's the case. . . . I'm very grateful. Yes, yes, it's more than enough. I'll give it back to you in three days.

OLGA PAVLOVNA

There, I'm glad. That'll be fine. There's no rush.

OSHIVENSKI

I'll leave you two alone. Thanks for the very pleasant chat, Mr. Kuznetsoff. I have to go down and discuss something with the landlady. *(hurries out)*

OLGA PAVLOVNA

Alyosha, forgive me if we ran into each other again. It's time for you to leave for the station, isn't it?

KUZNETSOFF

That radiant expression on your face. . . . Oh, Olya, Olya. . . .

OLGA PAVLOVNA

Naturally I'm glad it turned out this way. You're so funny. Do you have to leave at once?

KUZNETSOFF

Yes, in ten minutes. What in hell ever made me come to see that old grouch. Incidentally, you know, if he were younger I might actually have even been able to use him for some minor assignment. In tandem with Taubendorf, or something like that.

OLGA PAVLOVNA

Listen, let's not talk about trifles right now. When we were saying good-by before I restrained myself. But now I feel like rebelling a little.

KUZNETSOFF

You call my work a trifle? Then it's really true—you were lying to me?

OLGA PAVLOVNA

Alyosha, you know perfectly well I was lying to you. If you chose to ignore it, it's your business. Tomorrow, maybe, I'll regret that I blurted all this out to you. But right now I can't help it.

KUZNETSOFF
(smiling)
Olya, please, don't blurt.

OLGA PAVLOVNA

No, no—wait. We've already said good-by, haven't we?

You've left. Imagine that you've left. And right now you're only reminiscing about me. There's nothing more honest than reminiscence.

KUZNETSOFF

Olya, I'll tell you one more time: my work, to me, is. . . . Anyway, you know that without my having to tell you. But here's something you don't know: I've done things after which any personal life—affairs of the heart and so on—is impossible for me. . . .

OLGA PAVLOVNA

Oh, Alyosha, this is all silly nonsense. I'm sick and tired of it. Since fate decided we should meet now, I know what fate wants.

KUZNETSOFF

Last year, when I was in Russia, the following incident occurred. The Soviet sleuths got wind of something. I sensed that if I did not take resolute action they would eventually get to the bottom of it. And you know what I did? I deliberately let three people, minor pawns in my organization, go before the firing squad. Don't start thinking I regret it one bit. I don't. That gambit saved the whole project. I knew perfectly well that those people would accept the entire guilt, rather than betray the least detail of our work. And the trail vanished into thin air.

OLGA PAVLOVNA

That's all very frightening. But I fail to see how it can change anything. Even if you began forging bank notes, that wouldn't change anything. Really, Alyosha, let's talk like humans.

KUZNETSOFF

But how, with a life like that, can you expect me to have

room for any sentiments or attachments? And the main thing—and I've told you this already—is that I don't want anybody being afraid for me, thinking about me, waiting for me, agonizing if, because of some stupid quirk of fate. . . . What are you smiling for, Olya?—it's silly.

OLGA PAVLOVNA

If you didn't love me, you wouldn't care whether I was afraid for you or waiting for you. And, you see, I'll be much less afraid if you leave knowing that I love you. It's very funny: I love you a thousand times more than I did at first, when we were living together.

KUZNETSOFF

I've got to go. Oh, all right, Olya, I'll make a confession: it's not easy for me to sacrifice certain feelings. But for the moment the sacrifice has to be made. And now let's go. Walk me to my taxi.

OLGA PAVLOVNA

No, wait—first let's sit down a moment. In the old days we always used to sit down before departures. *(sits down on a wicker hamper)*

KUZNETSOFF

All right. Only don't smile like that. After all, one is supposed to remain silent.

OLGA PAVLOVNA

You're smiling too. . . . *(The clock strikes seven.)*

KUZNETSOFF

(getting up)
So. Time to go.

OLGA PAVLOVNA
(rushing to him)
And if I don't let you go? How can I live without you?

KUZNETSOFF
(placing his hands on her shoulders)
Olya, I'm going to the USSR so that you will be able to come to Russia. And everybody will be there. . . . Old Oshivenski living out his days, and Kolya Taubendorf, and that funny Fyodor Fyodorovich. Everybody.

OLGA PAVLOVNA
(pressing against him)
And you, Alyosha—where will *you* be?

KUZNETSOFF
(picks up his suitcase, puts the other arm around his wife, and both walk slowly toward the door; as they do so Kuznetsoff speaks gently and somewhat mysteriously.)
Listen—once upon a time there lived in Toulon an artillery officer, and that very same artillery officer—
(They leave.)

CURTAIN

The Event

A DRAMATIC COMEDY
IN THREE ACTS

INTRODUCTORY NOTE

The Event (Sobytie) was completed in 1938 in Menton, France. It was published in the émigré review *Russkie Zapiski (Annales russes),* Paris, for April 1938.

It was first produced by the "Russian Theatre," in Paris in March 1938. The director and set designer was the artist Yuri Annenkov. The play's originality provoked many echoes and much discussion in the émigré press. It played to a full theatre and had such success that there were several additional performances. It was staged, in Russian, in Prague in May of the same year, and in Warsaw and Belgrade in 1941. On 4 April 1941 it was put on in New York, again in Russian, at the Heckscher Theatre. G. S. Ermolov directed and played the part of Troshcheykin. The sets were by Dobuzhinsky, and included a splendid cracked plate and a counterfeit photo portrait, presumably of the Troshcheykins' dead child. These cardboard survivors now hang in Mother's parlor in Montreux.

The translation is literal with very minor adjustments only where the reader or theatregoer unfamiliar with the Russian idiom or the frame of reference would otherwise be hopelessly stumped.

CAST OF CHARACTERS

Alexéy (Alyósha) Maxímovich Troshchéykin, a portrait
  painter
Lyubóv' (Lyúba) Ivánovna Troshchéykin, his wife
Antonína Pávlovna Opayáshin, her mother
Ryóvshin
Véra, sister of Lyubóv'
Márfa, the maid
Eleonóra Kárlovna Shnap, a midwife
Mrs. Vagabúndov
Yevghénia Vasílyevna (Aunt Zhénya), aunt of Lyubóv' and
  Véra
Uncle Paul, her husband
The Famous Writer (Pyotr Nikoláevich)
Old Mrs. Nikoládze
Ígor Olégovich Kúprikov, an artist
The Reporter
Mesháev One (Ósip Mikhéyevich Mesháev)
Iván Ivánovich Shchel', a gun dealer
Ál'fred Afanásyevich Barbóshin, a private detective
Mesháev Two (Mikhéy Mikhéyevich Mesháev), Mesháev
  One's twin brother
Leoníd (Lyónya) Víctorovich Barbáshin (does not appear)
Arshínski (does not appear)

ACT ONE

Troshcheykin's studio. Doors on right and left [here, as in the original Russian text, stage directions are given from the audience's point of view]. On a low easel, in front of which is an armchair (Troshcheykin always works in a sitting position), stands a nearly finished portrait of a boy in blue, with five round blank spaces (future balls) arranged in a half circle at his feet. Against the wall leans an unfinished old woman in lace, with a white fan. A window, an ottoman, a scatter rug, a screen, a wardrobe, three chairs, two tables, portfolios piled up in disorder.

At first the stage is empty. Then a red-and-blue child's ball appears from the right and rolls slowly across. Through the same door enters Troshcheykin. With his foot he shuffles out another ball, this one red and yellow, from under the table. Troshcheykin is in his late thirties. He is clean-shaven and wears a shabby but colorful long-sleeved sweater that he does not remove for the entire length of the three acts (which represent, by the way, the morning, afternoon and evening of the same day). He is infantile, nervous, capricious.

TROSHCHEYKIN
Lyuba! *Lyuba!*

(Lyubov' comes in from left. She is young, pretty and seems a bit lazy and vague.)

TROSHCHEYKIN

What a *disaster!* How do these things happen? Why have those balls gone wandering off all over the house? It's scandalous. I refuse to spend all morning looking and bending. The kid is coming to pose today, and there are only *two* balls here. Where are the others?

LYUBOV'

How do I know? There was one in the hallway.

TROSHCHEYKIN

Here, this is the one that was in the hallway. The green one and the two speckled ones are missing. Vanished.

LYUBOV'

Will you please stop pestering me. After all, it isn't the end of the world. You can call your picture "Boy with Two Balls" instead of "Boy with Five Balls."

TROSHCHEYKIN

That's an intelligent suggestion. I would just like to know who actually spends his time scattering my props. . . . It's a disgrace.

LYUBOV'

You know as well as I that he was playing with them yesterday after his sitting.

TROSHCHEYKIN

In that case they should have been picked up afterwards and put where they belong. *(sits in front of the easel)*

LYUBOV'

What do I have to do with it? Tell Marfa. She's the one who does the housework.

TROSHCHEYKIN

And pretty badly too. I'm going to go give her a little lecture.

LYUBOV'

In the first place she has gone shopping, and in the second you're terrified of her.

TROSHCHEYKIN

Sure, that's quite possible. Although, personally, I'd always thought I was simply being courteous. That boy of mine isn't bad, though, is he? Just look at that velvet! I made his eyes so shiny partly because he is a jeweler's son.

LYUBOV'

I don't know why you can't paint in the balls first, and then finish the figure.

TROSHCHEYKIN

How can I explain it. . . .

LYUBOV'

You don't have to.

TROSHCHEYKIN

You see, the balls have to *glow,* to cast their reflection on him, but I want the reflection firmly in place before tackling its source. You must remember that art moves against the sun. See what a nice mother-of-pearl sheen his legs have already. I must admit I really like that portrait. The hair came out well, with that hint of black curliness. There is a certain connection between precious stones and Negro blood. Shakespeare sensed it in *Othello*. So. *(looks at the other portrait)* As for Madame Vagabundov she is extremely pleased that I am painting her in a white dress against a Spanish background, and does not understand what a horrid, lacy grotesque that makes. . . . I'd really like to ask you to look for those balls, though, Lyuba. I don't want them to remain in hiding.

LYUBOV'

This is cruel—unbearable, even. Lock them in the closet, for God's sake. I can't have things rolling around the rooms and crawling under the furniture either. Really, Alyosha, don't you see *why?*

TROSHCHEYKIN

What's the matter with you? Why this tone? . . . Why the hysterics?

LYUBOV'

Certain things are torture for me.

TROSHCHEYKIN

What things?

LYUBOV'

These toy balls, for one thing. I. Can't. Stand. It. It's Mother's birthday today—that means day after tomorrow he would have been five. *Five*—just think.

TROSHCHEYKIN

So that's it. . . . Well, you know. . . . Lyuba, Lyuba—I've told you a thousand times it's not possible to live in the conditional like this. Five years, then another five, and so on,

then he would have been fifteen and would have smoked
and been rude and had acne and peeked into ladies'
décolletés.

LYUBOV'

Want to know what I sometimes ask myself? Do you realize
you are monstrously gross?

TROSHCHEYKIN

And you're as rude as a fishwife. *(pause—approaching her)*
Come on, come on, don't go into a huff. . . . Maybe my heart
is breaking, too, but I know how to control myself. Look at it
sensibly—he died at two, he folded his little wings and fell
like a stone into the depths of our souls, and if he hadn't he
would have grown and grown, and developed into a
nincompoop.

LYUBOV'

I implore you, stop it! Don't you realize this is so vulgar it's
frightening! The way you talk gives me a toothache.

TROSHCHEYKIN

Relax, old girl. That'll be enough. If I say something wrong,
forgive me and pity me instead of snapping at me. By the
way, I hardly got any sleep last night.

LYUBOV'

Liar.

TROSHCHEYKIN

I knew you would say that!

LYUBOV'

Liar. You did not know.

TROSHCHEYKIN

Still, it's true. In the first place, I always get palpitations when there is a full moon. And then I've been getting these shooting pains here every now and then—I don't know what's happening to me. . . . And all kinds of thoughts, too—my eyes are closed, but there is such a merry-go-round of colors spinning in my head I could go insane. Give me a smile, Lyuba, my dove.

LYUBOV'

Leave me alone.

TROSHCHEYKIN

(on the proscenium)

Listen, pet, let me tell you about an idea I had last night. I think it's quite a stroke of genius. Here's what I'd like to paint—try to imagine that this wall is missing, and instead there is a black abyss and what looks like an audience in a dim theater, rows and rows of faces, sitting and watching me. And all the faces belong to people whom I know or once knew, and who are now watching my life. Some with curiosity, some with vexation, some with pleasure. This man with envy; that woman with compassion. There they sit before me, so pale and wondrous in the semidarkness. My late parents are there, and my past enemies, and that character of yours with his gun, and my childhood friends, of course, and lots and lots of women—all the ones I told you about: Nina, Ada, Katyúsha, the other Nina, Margaret Hoffman, poor Ólenka—all of them. What do you think of it?

LYUBOV'

How should I know? Paint it, then I'll tell you.

TROSHCHEYKIN

Then again, maybe it's all nonsense, just a fleeting image

seen in a semidelirious state, a surrogate for insomnia,
sickroom art. . . . Let there be a wall again.

LYUBOV'

About seven people are coming for tea today. You'd better
tell me what to buy.

TROSHCHEYKIN

*(who has sat down and is holding, propped on one knee, a charcoal
sketch, which he examines, then begins to touch up)*
What a bore. Who's coming?

LYUBOV'

I, too, have a list for you. First of all, His Authorial
Majesty — I don't know why Mama[1] wanted at all costs that he
honor her with a visit; he has never been to our house before,
and they say he is arrogant and obnoxious. . . .

TROSHCHEYKIN

Yeah. . . . You know how fond I am of your mama and
how delighted I am that she is living with us. Rather than
in some cozy little room with a clock that goes tick-tock
and one of those dachshunds, perhaps even no more than
a couple of blocks away — but forgive me, pet, if I say
that her most recent opus, in yesterday's paper, is a
catastrophe.

LYUBOV'

That's not what I wanted to know. I asked you what I should
get for tea.

---

[1] For English-language productions, the last syllable of "Mama" should
be stressed.

TROSHCHEYKIN

It makes no difference to me. Ab-so-lute-ly none. I don't even want to think about it. Get whatever you want. A strawberry cake, say. And lots of oranges—you know, the sour but nice-looking ones: that immediately brightens up the whole table. Champagne we have, and candy will come with the guests.

LYUBOV'

I'd like to know where I'm supposed to find oranges in August. Incidentally, this is all we have by way of money. We owe the butcher, we owe Marfa, and I don't know how we are going to make ends meet until the next time you get paid.

TROSHCHEYKIN

I repeat again that the matter is totally indifferent to me. How boring, Lyuba, how sad! For five years now we've been languishing in this super-provincial town, where I think I have daubed every paterfamilias, every round-heeled little housewife, every dentist, every gynecologist. Things are going from ludicrous to plain lewd. By the way, you know, I used my double-portrait method again the other day. It's pretty damned amusing. Unbeknownst to Baumgarten I painted two versions of him simultaneously on the sly: on one canvas as the dignified elder he wanted, and on another the way *I* wanted him—purple mug, bronze belly, surrounded by thunderclouds. Of course I didn't show him the second, but gave it to Kuprikov. When I accumulate twenty or so of these by-products, I'll exhibit them.

LYUBOV'

All of your plans have one remarkable peculiarity: they are always like half-open doors that slam shut with the first gust of wind.

TROSHCHEYKIN

Well, what do you know. How clever we are at observing things and at expressing them! Well, dear girl, if that were so, you and I would have starved to death long ago.

LYUBOV'

And you're not going to get away with calling me a fish-wife.

TROSHCHEYKIN

We start squabbling first thing in the morning, and it's tedious beyond words. Today I deliberately got up early to get something finished and start on something new. How nice. Your foul mood has made me lose all desire to work. I hope you're satisfied.

LYUBOV'

You ought to stop and think how it started today. No, Alyosha, we can't go on like this. . . . You keep living under the illusion that time heals all wounds, as they say, while I know that it is only a palliative, if not outright quackery. I can forget nothing, while you do not want to remember anything. If I see a toy, and it brings back the memory of my baby, you get bored and vexed, because you have reached an agreement with yourself that after three years it's time to forget. And perhaps even—Heaven only knows—perhaps you have nothing to forget.

TROSHCHEYKIN

Nonsense. . . . What on earth has gotten into you? First of all, I never said anything of the sort, but simply that we cannot expect to exist forever by collecting life's old debts. There's nothing either vulgar or insulting about that.

LYUBOV'
Never mind. Let's not talk about it anymore.

TROSHCHEYKIN
Suit yourself. *(pause. He sprays the sketch with a fixing agent by blowing into a special jar, then starts on something else.)* No, I don't understand you at all. And you don't understand yourself. The point is that we are decaying in this hick-town atmosphere, like Chekhov's three sisters. No matter. . . . In a year or so we'll have to get out of here, like it or not. Don't know why there's no answer from that Italian. . . .
(Antonina Pavlovna Opayashin, Lyubov's mother, comes in with a speckled ball. She is a neat, even slightly prim, mawkish and absentminded lady with a lorgnette.)

ANTONINA PAVLOVNA
Hello, my dears. For some reason this ended up in my room. Thank you, Alyosha, for the lovely flowers.

TROSHCHEYKIN
(He does not look up from his work throughout this whole scene.)
Happy birthday, happy birthday. Here, in the corner, please.

LYUBOV'
You got up early, didn't you? I don't think it's even nine o'clock yet.

ANTONINA PAVLOVNA
I was born early, I guess. Had your coffee yet?

LYUBOV'
Yes. Perhaps, in honor of your fiftieth birthday, you'll have some too?

TROSHCHEYKIN

Incidentally, Antonina Pavlovna, do you know who else has three-fifths of a carrot in the morning like you?

ANTONINA PAVLOVNA

Who?

TROSHCHEYKIN

Don't know. I was asking *you.*

LYUBOV'

Alyosha is in a nice, jocular mood today. Well, Mummy, what would you like to do before lunch? Would you like to take a walk with me? To the lake, or to have a look at the animals?

ANTONINA PAVLOVNA

What animals?

LYUBOV'

There's a traveling circus on the vacant lot.

TROSHCHEYKIN

I'll join you. I love circuses. I might pick up a horse's croup or an old clown in street clothes.

ANTONINA PAVLOVNA

No, I had better do some work in the morning. Vérochka will probably drop in. . . . It's strange I haven't heard from Misha. . . . You know, children, last night I scribbled another one of those fantasies for the *Illumined Lakes* cycle.

LYUBOV'

Marvelous. Look what a miserable day it is out. Can't tell

whether it's raining or just misty. Hard to believe it's still summer. By the way, did you notice that in the mornings Marfa quite brazenly takes your umbrella?

ANTONINA PAVLOVNA

She just got back and is in a tetchy mood. Unpleasant to talk to. Want to hear my little fairy tale? Or am I disturbing your work, Alyosha?

TROSHCHEYKIN

Oh, you know, even an earthquake won't distract me once I get started. But now I'm just fiddling around. Shoot.

ANTONINA PAVLOVNA

Maybe you people aren't interested?

LYUBOV'

Oh, no, Mummy. Of course we are—do read it.

TROSHCHEYKIN

Tell me something, Antonina Pavlovna, why did you invite our Venerable Master? I keep racking my brain over it. What do you need him for? What's a chessboard with one queen and a lot of pawns?

ANTONINA PAVLOVNA

They're not pawns at all. There's Meshaev, for instance—

TROSHCHEYKIN

Meshaev? Well, I must say. . . .

LYUBOV'

Mummy, don't answer him. What's the use?

ANTONINA PAVLOVNA

I only wanted to say that Meshaev, for instance, promised he would bring his brother, who is an occultist.

TROSHCHEYKIN

He has no brother. That is a mystification.

ANTONINA PAVLOVNA

Yes, he has. Only the brother always lives in the country. They are even twins.

TROSHCHEYKIN

Yeah, I'll bet they are.

LYUBOV'

Well, when are we going to hear your story?

ANTONINA PAVLOVNA

Oh, never mind. Some other time.

LYUBOV'

Don't be hurt, Mummy. Alyosha!

TROSHCHEYKIN

I'm standing in for him.
(The doorbell rings.)

ANTONINA PAVLOVNA

No, no—it's all right: I'll type it up first, otherwise it's not very legible.

LYUBOV'

Type it up and then come read it. Please!

TROSHCHEYKIN
Second the motion.

ANTONINA PAVLOVNA
You're sure? All right, then I'll be back in a moment.
(On her way out, just beyond the door, she bumps into Ryovshin, who is first heard, then seen: he is a foppish, wriggly fellow with a short black beard and whiskery eyebrows. His coworkers have dubbed him The Hairy Helminth.)

RYOVSHIN
(on the other side of the door)
And is Alexey Maximovich up? Alive and well? Everything fine? Actually, it's him I'd like to see for a moment. *(to Troshcheykin)* May I come in?

TROSHCHEYKIN
By all means, good sir.

RYOVSHIN
Hello, luv. . . . Hello, Alexey Maximovich. Everything shipshape with you?

TROSHCHEYKIN
How solicitous he is, eh? Yes, finances apart, everything is first-rate.

RYOVSHIN
Excuse me for barging in at such an ungodly hour. I was passing by and thought I'd say hello.

LYUBOV'
Will you have some coffee?

RYOVSHIN

No, I thank you. I just dropped in for a minute. Oh, I think I forgot to wish your mama a happy birthday. How embarrassing. . . .

TROSHCHEYKIN

How come you are so nervous and cocky at the same time today?

RYOVSHIN

No, no—what are you saying—? *(pause)* So that's the way it is. *(pause)* Did you stay home last night?

LYUBOV'

Yes, why?

RYOVSHIN

Just asking. So that's how things are, then. . . . Are you sketching?

TROSHCHEYKIN

No, I'm playing the harp. Come on, sit down someplace. *(pause)*

RYOVSHIN

It's drizzling out.

TROSHCHEYKIN

How very interesting. Any other news?

RYOVSHIN

Oh, no, none at all. I just dropped in. You know, today, I was walking and thinking: how long have we known each other,

Alexey Maximovich? Seven years, isn't it?

LYUBOV'
I'd very much like to know what has happened.

RYOVSHIN
Oh, just trifles. You know, business complications.

TROSHCHEYKIN
You're right, pet. He is kind of twitchy today. Maybe you have fleas? How about a bath?

RYOVSHIN
You never stop kidding, do you, Alexey Maximovich? No. I was just reminiscing about the days when I was your best man and so forth. There are days when one reminisces.

LYUBOV'
What's wrong—is your conscience bothering you?

RYOVSHIN
There are days like that. . . . Time flies. . . . You look back, and—

TROSHCHEYKIN
Oh, how boring this is getting. . . . Why don't you step into the library, good sir, and brush up on your reading? This afternoon our Venerable Master is coming. I'm willing to bet he'll arrive in a dinner jacket as at the Vishnév-skis'.

RYOVSHIN
At the Vishnevskis'? Oh, yes, of course. . . . You know, Lyubov'

Ivanovna, I think I'll have a little cup of coffee after all.

LYUBOV'
Thank heavens! You finally made up your mind. *(goes out)*

RYOVSHIN
Listen, Alexey Maximovich—something sensational has happened! A sensationally unpleasant event.

TROSHCHEYKIN
Are you serious?

RYOVSHIN
I don't even know how to tell you. Just don't get excited— and, above all, Lyubov' Ivanovna must know nothing for the time being.

TROSHCHEYKIN
What is it, some vile gossip?

RYOVSHIN
Worse.

TROSHCHEYKIN
Namely?

RYOVSHIN
Something unforeseen and horrible, Alexey Maximovich.

TROSHCHEYKIN
Well, out with it then, damn you!

RYOVSHIN
Barbashin is back.

TROSHCHEYKIN
What?

RYOVSHIN
Last night. They lopped a year and a half off his sentence.

TROSHCHEYKIN
It can't be!

RYOVSHIN
Just don't get excited. We must discuss it, and work out some kind of *modus vivendi.*

TROSHCHEYKIN
Vivendi my foot. To hell with *vivendi.* But . . . but . . . *What will happen now?* Good Lord. . . . You must be kidding—you are, aren't you?

RYOVSHIN
Get a firm grip on yourself. You and I had better find some place to. . . .
(Lyubov' re-enters.)

LYUBOV'
You'll be served in a moment. By the way, Alyosha, she says the fruit—Alyosha, what happened?

TROSHCHEYKIN
The inevitable.

RYOVSHIN
Alexey Maximovich, Alyosha, my friend—let's go out for a while now. The fresh morning air will make your headache go away, and you can walk me home. . . .

LYUBOV'

I want to know this instant. Did someone die?

TROSHCHEYKIN

It's monstrously funny, though. Poor idiot that I am, a moment ago I still had a year and a half in reserve. By that time we would have long since been in a different city, in a different country, on a different planet. I don't understand: what is this, a trap? Why didn't anybody warn us beforehand? What kind of rotten way of running things is this? Where did these tenderhearted judges come from? The *bastards*! Just think—they let him out early! No, it's ... it's ... I'll lodge a complaint! I'll—

RYOVSHIN

Take it easy, old man.

LYUBOV'

(to Ryovshin)

Is this true?

RYOVSHIN

Is what true?

LYUBOV'

No, no, don't raise your eyebrows. You know perfectly well what I mean.

TROSHCHEYKIN

I'd very much like to know who stands to benefit from this indulgence. *(to Ryovshin)* Why don't you say something? Did you talk to him? . . .

RYOVSHIN

Yes.

LYUBOV'
And how is he—very much changed?

TROSHCHEYKIN
Lyuba, enough of your idiotic questions. Don't you realize what'll happen now? We have to run, and there's no place to run to, and no money to do it with. *What* a surprise!

LYUBOV'
Come on, tell us.

TROSHCHEYKIN
Yes, indeed, why sit there like a stone statue. Come on, stop torturing us.

RYOVSHIN
To make a long story short. . . . Last night, towards midnight, at ten-forty-five or so, I'd say . . . nonsense, what am I talking about? I mean eleven-forty-five . . . I was walking home from the cinema across the square from you . . . and, can you believe it, right there, just a few steps from your house, but on the other side of the street, you know, by the newsstand—I couldn't believe my eyes—there, in the light of a street lamp, smoking a cigarette, stood Barbashin.

TROSHCHEYKIN
Right on our corner! Delightful! And you and I, Lyuba, nearly went, too: great film, you said, *Camera Obscura,* you said, highlight of the season. Instead of the highlight, it would have been lights out for us. Go on!

RYOVSHIN
Now then. We never had seen much of each other, and he

might have forgotten what I looked like, but no—he gave me a piercing glance—you know, one of those haughty, derisive glances of his, and I could not help stopping. We said hello. I was curious, of course. "How is it," I asked, "that you're back in our bailiwick so prematurely?"

LYUBOV'

You mean you came right out like that and asked him?

RYOVSHIN

Anyway, words to that effect. I mumbled something, improvised a few phrases of greeting, and let him take it from there, of course. And indeed he did. "Yes," he says, "because of my exemplary conduct, and on the occasion of an official celebration, I was asked to vacate my government-assigned quarters a year and a half early." And he looks at me. Insolently.

TROSHCHEYKIN

The son of a bitch. Eh? Can anyone please tell me what's going on? Where are we, in Corsica? What is this, an incitement to vendetta?

LYUBOV'

(to Ryovshin)

And at this point you apparently got the jitters.

RYOVSHIN

Not a bit. "What," I asked, "do you plan to do now?" "To live," he says, "live for my own pleasure," and he looks at me, laughing. "And why, sir," I ask, "are you loitering around here in the dark?" . . . That is, I didn't say it out loud, but just thought it most eloquently. I hope he got the message. And with that, well—we parted.

TROSHCHEYKIN

You're not so hot yourself. Why didn't you drop in immediately? Who knows, I might have gone out to mail a letter, and then what would have happened? You could at least have taken the trouble to phone me.

RYOVSHIN

Well, you know, it was kind of late. . . . I said to myself, let them get a good night's sleep.

TROSHCHEYKIN

I didn't feel particularly sleepy, and now I know why!

RYOVSHIN

I also noticed that he reeked of perfume. This, on top of his sarcastic surliness, struck me as being downright satanic.

TROSHCHEYKIN

Everything is clear. There is nothing to discuss. . . . Everything is *perfectly* clear. I'm going to get the entire police force jumping! I will not stand for this benevolence! I refuse to understand *how*, after his threats, about which everybody knew and knows, *how*, after that, they could have allowed him to return to this city!

LYUBOV'

It was only something he shouted in a moment of excitement.

TROSHCHEYKIN

'Xitement, 'xitement! I like that! Sorry, dear girl, but when a man starts shooting, sees he hasn't killed his victims outright, and screams that he will finish the job as soon as he's served his sentence—that's . . . that's not excitement, but fact, bloody, fleshy fact, that's what it is! What an ass I was. They said seven years, and I believed them. I thought calmly, four more years, three more, a year and a half, and, when there is only half a year left, we'll get out of here no matter what. . . . I'd already begun writing to my friend in Capri to make arrangements. . . . Lord, I deserve to be thrashed!

RYOVSHIN

Let's keep cool, Alexey Maximovich. It's essential to remain lucid and unafraid . . . though caution, even supreme caution, is imperative. I'll be frank: according to my observations, he is in a state of extreme anger and tension, and forced labor has not tamed him in the least. As I said before, I may be mistaken.

LYUBOV'

Except that forced labor has nothing to do with it. The man was in jail, that's all.

TROSHCHEYKIN

All this is *horrible.*

RYOVSHIN

Here, then, is my plan: at about ten o'clock, you and I, Alexey Maximovich, will go over to Vishnevski's office. Since he was your lawyer at the time, we must first of all see him. It's perfectly obvious to anyone that you can't go on living under a threat like this. . . . Forgive me if I evoke painful memories, but it happened in this very room, didn't it?

TROSHCHEYKIN

Exactly, exactly. Of course this was all forgotten, and Madame, here, would get annoyed when I recalled it jokingly now and then. . . . It seemed like something we'd seen at the theatre, in some melodrama. I even sometimes . . . yes, it was to *you* that I showed a spot of carmine paint on the floor with the witty comment that the trace of blood was still there. Clever joke.

RYOVSHIN
Right here in this room, then? Tsk, tsk, tsk.

LYUBOV'
Yes, in this room.

TROSHCHEYKIN
In this very room. We had just moved in: real newlyweds, I with my mustache, she with her flowers—the whole bit. A touching spectacle. We didn't have that wardrobe then, and this one stood by the wall over there, but everything else was the same then as now, even that little rug. . . .

RYOVSHIN
Amazing!

TROSHCHEYKIN
Not amazing, but criminal. Yesterday, today, everything was so peaceful. . . . And now look at us! What can I do? I don't have the money either to defend myself or to flee. How could they set him free, after all that happened. . . . Look, this is how it was. I was sitting here. No, wait—the table was in a different spot, too. Here, I believe. You see—memory does not immediately adjust to a repeat performance. Yesterday it all seemed so long ago. . . .

LYUBOV'
It was October eighth, and raining, because I remember the

ambulance attendants' cloaks were wet, and my face felt wet too as they were carrying me. You might find that detail useful for your reconstruction.

RYOVSHIN

What an amazing thing is memory!

TROSHCHEYKIN

Here, the furniture is correctly positioned now. Yes, October eighth. Her brother, Mikhaíl Ivánovich, was visiting us and stayed the night. So. It was evening. Outside it was already dark. I was sitting *here* by the little table, peeling an apple. Like this. She was sitting over there, where she stands now. Suddenly the doorbell rings. We had a new maid, a blockhead even worse than Marfa. I look up and see Barbashin standing in the doorway. Here, stand by the door. All the way back. There. Lyuba and I rise automatically, and he immediately opens fire.

RYOVSHIN

Just think. . . . It's not even twenty feet from here to there.

TROSHCHEYKIN

Not even twenty feet? The very first shot hits her in the hip, and she sits down on the floor, and the second zaps me in the left hand—here—another half inch and it would have splintered the bone. He keeps firing, and there I stand with my apple, like a young William Tell. At that moment . . . at that moment my brother-in-law comes in and piles on him from behind; you remember him—huge bear of a man. Grabs him and puts a hammerlock on him. While I, in spite of my wound and the terrible pain, calmly go up to Barbashin and whack him on the kisser. . . . That's when he shouted it—I remember every word: "Just wait, I'll be back to finish off both of you!"

RYOVSHIN
I recall how the late Margarita Semyonovna Hoffman gave me the news. I was flabbergasted. Worst of all, the rumor somehow started that Lyubov' Ivanovna was on the point of death.

LYUBOV'
Actually, of course, it was just a trifle. I was laid up for a couple of weeks, no more. Now you can't even see the scar.

TROSHCHEYKIN
Whoa, there—you can see it all right. And it wasn't two weeks, but over a month. Now, now, I remember it perfectly well. My hand was no laughing matter either. This is all so, so.... And on top of it all I busted my watch yesterday, damn it! Is it time to go yet?

RYOVSHIN
There's no point in going before ten: he comes into the office at about ten-fifteen. Or else we could go right to his house—it's practically next door. Which do you prefer?

TROSHCHEYKIN
I'll go phone him at home right away, that's what I'll do. *(goes out)*

LYUBOV'
Tell me, has Barbashin changed much?

RYOVSHIN

Oh, cut it out, Lyubikins.[2] A mug like any other mug.
(a short pause)
What a mess! You know, I feel very, very uneasy inside, kind
of itchy.

LYUBOV'

Never mind, let it itch—a little massage is good for the soul.
Just don't you start meddling.

RYOVSHIN

If I meddle, it's exclusively for your sake. I am amazed
by your calmness! And to think I was all set to prepare
you for the news—I was afraid you'd have a fit of
hysterics.

LYUBOV'

I apologize. I'll have one next time for your benefit.

RYOVSHIN

Tell me, though—do you think I should have a heart-to-
heart talk with him?

LYUBOV'

Heart-to-heart with whom?

RYOVSHIN

Why, with Barbashin. Maybe if I were to tell him that your
conjugal bliss is nothing to brag about—

[2] Although generally Russian diminutives have been left unchanged, this
exception has been made because it renders well the special flavor that
"Lyubka" has here.

LYUBOV'
Heart-to-heart indeed! You just try. He'll take you apart for
your heart-to-heart.

RYOVSHIN
Don't get mad. Don't you see? It's just plain logic. If he tried
to murder you *then*, because you were happy with your
husband, now he would have no reason for it.

LYUBOV'
Especially since now we have our little affair going, isn't that
right? Go on, tell him about it. Just try.

RYOVSHIN
Oh, well, you know—after all, I am a gentleman. But even if
he were to find out, believe me, he wouldn't give a hoot. It's
on a completely different plane.

LYUBOV'
Try, just try.

RYOVSHIN
Don't get mad. I only wanted to help. Oh, I'm so upset.

LYUBOV'
None of it makes a single bit of difference to me. If you all
only knew how little difference it makes. . . . And where is he
staying? Same place as before?

RYOVSHIN
Yes, apparently. You don't love me today.

LYUBOV'
I never did love you, my dear. Never. Is that clear?

RYOVSHIN

Sweetie-pie, don't say that. It's sinful!

LYUBOV'

And why don't you talk a little louder? That would really fix things.

RYOVSHIN

As if darling Alyosha didn't know! He's known for a long time, and doesn't give a hoot.

LYUBOV'

You and all your hooting. No, today I absolutely cannot face discussions like this. I greatly appreciate that you came running right over with your tongue lolling to tell, to share, etcetera, but now please leave.

RYOVSHIN

Yes, I'll be leaving with him in a moment. Would you rather I waited in the dining room? He's probably telling the whole story all over again on the phone. *(pause)* Sweetie-pie, I tearfully beg you, please stay home today. If you need anything, just tell me. And Marfa must be warned, so she won't let him in.

LYUBOV'

You really think he's going to come visiting? To wish my mummy happy birthday? Or what?

RYOVSHIN

No, no, just in case, until things get cleared up.

LYUBOV'

Just don't you go clearing anything up.

RYOVSHIN

That's a good one. You're putting me in an impossible position.

LYUBOV'

No matter—be content with the impossible. It won't last much longer.

RYOVSHIN

I'm miserable, hairy, and boring. Come on right out and say it—you're fed up with me.

LYUBOV'

All right. I am.

RYOVSHIN

And you are the most exquisite, strange, enchanting creature in the whole world. You were conceived by Chekhov, written by Rostand, and acted by Duse. No, no, no! Once bestowed, happiness cannot be withdrawn. Listen, would you like me to challenge Barbashin to a duel?

LYUBOV'

Stop clowning. How revolting! You'd better put this table back where it belongs. I keep bumping into it. You come in running and panting and get poor Alyosha all upset. . . . What was the need for it? "Kill," "finish off," "slaughter"— what kind of drivel is this?

RYOVSHIN

Let's hope that it is drivel.

LYUBOV'

Then again maybe he *will* kill us. Who can tell?

RYOVSHIN

See, you envisage the possibility yourself.

LYUBOV'

Listen, my dear, I envisage a lot of things, including some
you don't even dream of.
(Troshcheykin returns.)

TROSHCHEYKIN

It's all taken care of. I've arranged the appointment. Come
on, he's expecting us at home.

RYOVSHIN

Had a nice long chat with him, didn't you?

TROSHCHEYKIN

Oh, I made another call too. Looks like we'll be able to
scrounge a little cash. Lyuba, your sister is here. We must
warn her and Antonina Pavlovna. If I get it, we'll shove off
tomorrow.

RYOVSHIN

Well, I see you're full of moxie. Maybe it's all wasted,
and Barbashin is not in such a passion. See, it even
rhymes.

TROSHCHEYKIN

No, no, it's best if we scoot off somewhere and think things
over once we're there. Anyway, everything is falling into place.
Listen, I've called a taxi — I don't much feel like walking. Come
on, let's go.

RYOVSHIN

Only don't expect me to pay for it.

TROSHCHEYKIN
I certainly do. What are you looking for? Here it is. Let's go.
Don't you worry, Lyuba—I'll be home in ten minutes.

LYUBOV'
I'm not worried at all. You'll come back alive.

RYOVSHIN
You just sit in your bower and be a good girl. I'll drop by
again this afternoon. Give me your little paw.
*(The two of them exit right while Vera appears unhurriedly from
the left. She is also young and attractive, but gentler and tamer than
her sister.)*

VERA
Hi. What's going on in this house?

LYUBOV'
Why?

VERA
I don't know. There's something a little rabid about
Alyosha's appearance. Are they gone?

LYUBOV'
They're gone.

VERA
Mama is tapping on her typewriter like a bunny on a drum.
(pause) It's raining again. Depressing day. Look, I got some
new gloves. Nice and cheap.

LYUBOV'
I have something new, too.

VERA

Oh, that's interesting.

LYUBOV'

Leonid is back.

VERA

Wow!

LYUBOV'

He has been seen on our corner.

VERA

No wonder I dreamt about him last night.

LYUBOV'

It seems they let him out of jail early.

VERA

It's strange, though: I dreamed that somebody locked him in a wardrobe, and when they started shaking it and trying to open it, he himself came running with a picklock, all in a dither, began helping, and when they finally opened the door there was nothing but a tailcoat hanging inside. Strange, isn't it?

LYUBOV'

Yes. Alyosha is in a blue funk.

VERA

What amazing news, Lyúbochka! Wouldn't it be fascinating to take a look at him? Remember how he always used to tease me, and how furious I would get? Actually I envied you terribly. Don't cry, Lyubochka. It'll all work out. I'm certain he won't kill you and Alyosha. Jail isn't a thermos jug in which you can keep the same idea hot indefinitely. Don't cry, honey.

LYUBOV'

There's a limit up to which. My nerves can hold out. But that limit. Has. Been passed.

VERA

Come on, please don't. After all, there are laws, there is the police, there's plain common sense. You'll see: he'll wander around for a while, heave a sigh, and disappear.

LYUBOV'

Oh, that's not the point. He can go ahead and kill me, I'd only be grateful. Do you have a handkerchief? Oh, dear Lord. . . . You know, today I was thinking about my baby—I could just see him playing with those balls—and Alyosha was so vile, so ghastly!

VERA

Yes, I know. If I were you I would have gotten a divorce long ago.

LYUBOV'

Do you have some powder? Thanks.

VERA

I would have gotten a divorce, married Ryovshin, and probably gotten another divorce right away.

LYUBOV'

When he came running in today with that phony air of a faithful dog and told us about it—everything, my whole life, burst into flames before my very eyes and burned up like a scrap of paper. Six absolutely useless years. The only bit of happiness was my child, and it died, too.

VERA

Come on, you were head over heels in love with Alyosha in the beginning.

LYUBOV'

Nonsense! I was just playacting for my own benefit. Nothing more. There was only one man whom I loved.

VERA

You know, I'm curious whether he'll get in touch or not. After all, sooner or later you're bound to run into him on the street.

LYUBOV'

There's one thing. . . . The way Alyosha hit him on the cheek while Misha was holding him. The way he took advantage. That thought always gave me a burning sense of anguish, and now it burns more than ever. Perhaps it's because I sense that Lyonya will never forgive me for having seen it.

VERA

What a crazy time that was anyway! God, remember what a state you were in when you decided to break up with him? Do you?

LYUBOV'

Really stupid thing to do, wasn't it? What an idiot I was.

VERA

You and I were sitting in a dusky garden, and stars were

falling, and we were both ghostlike in our white dresses, and the scented tobacco flowers were blooming in the flower bed, and you were saying you couldn't stand it any longer, that Lyonya was squeezing you dry—those were your very words.

LYUBOV'

Indeed, I do remember. He had a terrible temper. He himself used to admit that it wasn't a temper but a distemper. He plagued me endlessly, senselessly with his jealousy, his moods, all his various quirks. And yet, that was the most wonderful time of my life.

VERA

And remember how Father used to say, in a tone of alarm, that he was involved in dubious dealings, that half his life was shady, and the other half shaky.

LYUBOV'

Oh, come, there was never any proof of that. It was just that everybody was terribly envious of Lyonya, and Father simply believed that if someone was involved in financial operations without actually buying or selling anything, he belonged either behind the bars of a bank or behind the bars of a jail. And Lyonya was a law unto himself.

VERA

Yes, but that also influenced you at the time.

LYUBOV'

Everybody began pressuring me. Massive Misha leaned on me with all his weight. Mama gnawed at me surreptitiously, as a dog chews on a doll when no one is looking. Only you, my darling, took it all in your stride and showed no surprise.

The main thing, though, was what was happening to me: when, after a tryst in the park, I imagined what life would be like under the same roof with him, felt it would be unendurable—the constant tension, the constant electricity in the air. . . . I was such an idiot!

VERA

And remember how he would arrive all glum, and glumly tell some story that would have us in stitches. Or how the three of us used to sit on the veranda, and I knew you two were dying for me to go, and I would sit in the rocking chair reading Turgenev, and you two on the couch, and I knew that the moment I left you would start kissing and did not go for that reason.

LYUBOV'

Yes, he loved me madly, with a madly unlucky love. There were other moments too, though, moments of perfect serenity.

VERA

When Father died, and the house and garden were sold, it hurt me that all the whispers, the jokes, and the tears its various nooks and crannies had known were somehow being sold along with it.

LYUBOV'

Yes, the tears, the chills. . . . He left for a couple of months on a business trip, and that's when Alyosha turned up, with his dreams, and his jars of paint. I pretended I was swept off my feet, and then, too, there was something pathetic about Alyosha. He was so childish, so helpless. That's when I wrote Lyonya that awful letter; remember how, in the middle of the night, you and I gazed at the mailbox within which it already lay, and had the sensation that the box was swelling, and in a minute would explode like a bomb.

VERA

Personally, I was never terribly impressed with Alyosha. I thought, though, that you would have a wonderfully interesting life with him, and now we still don't really know whether he is a great artist or a nothing. "My ancestor," he said to me, "a military governor in the fourteenth century, spelled his name with a 'y'[3], and therefore, dear Vera, I request that henceforth you spell my name the same way."

LYUBOV'

Yes, and the end result is that I got married to a "y." And I haven't the vaguest idea what's going to happen next. . . . And can you please tell me why I had to have that free supplement with Ryovshin? What do I need it for? It only means an extra burden on my soul and extra dust in the house. And how humiliating it all is, with Alyosha perfectly aware of the whole thing and pretending that everything is hunky-dory between us. My God, Verochka, just think: right now Lyonya is just a few blocks away, and my imagination keeps rushing there, but sees nothing.
(Marfa enters with two balls.)

VERA

In any case, this is all absolutely fascinating.
(Marfa takes away the coffee cup.)

MARFA

What should I buy for tea? Or are you going out yourself?

---

[3] In the Russian, the play is on the now abolished letter "yat'" and is untranslatable literally.

LYUBOV'

No, I'd rather you did, please. Or else couldn't we order by phone? I don't know—in a moment I'll come and tell you.
(Troshcheykin runs in. Marfa goes out.)

LYUBOV'

Well?

TROSHCHEYKIN

All right for now. The city is quiet.

VERA

What did you expect people to do, Alyosha, start parading with flags?

TROSHCHEYKIN

What was that? What flags? *(to his wife)* Does she know already?
(Lyubov' gives a shrug.)

TROSHCHEYKIN

(to Vera)

Well, what do you say? Pleasant situation, isn't it?

VERA

I think it's marvelous.

TROSHCHEYKIN

You can congratulate me. I quarreled at once with Vishnevski. That old toad! It's no skin off his back. He called the police, but it still isn't clear whether or not there is any protection, and, if there is, what it consists of. What it boils down to is that nobody can do anything until we've been murdered. In a word, it's all very nice and elegant. By the way, from the taxi a moment ago I saw his sidekick—what's his name?—Arshinski. A bad sign.

VERA

Oh, you saw Arshinski? Is he here? I haven't seen him in a thousand years. Yes, it's true that he was a great friend of Lyonya Barbashin's.

TROSHCHEYKIN

He was another one of those gloomy scoundrels—he and Lyonya Barbashin cooked up counterfeit I.O.U.'s together. Listen, Lyuba, since we'll need money for the trip, I don't want to miss any sittings today. The kid is coming at two, and after that the old woman, and of course we must cancel the guests—you please take care of it.

LYUBOV'

Don't be funny. On the contrary, I'm going to take care of the cake now. This is Mama's birthday, and I don't have the least intention of spoiling it for her because of some silly ghosts.

TROSHCHEYKIN

Dearest, these ghosts *kill*. Do you understand this or not? If you treat danger in general with such birdbrained levity, then . . . I just don't know. . . .

VERA

Alyosha, are you afraid he'll slip in with the others?

TROSHCHEYKIN

That would be reason enough. There's nothing funny about

it. Par-ty time! Isn't that nice! When the fortress is in a state
of *siege* you don't ask your dear friends to come visiting.

LYUBOV'
Alyosha, the fortress has already surrendered.

TROSHCHEYKIN
Are you doing it on purpose? Are you determined to drive
me bananas?

LYUBOV'
No, but I simply don't want to ruin other people's lives
because of your whims.

TROSHCHEYKIN
There are a thousand things to decide, and we're spending
our time on ridiculous nonsense. Let's assume that Baumgarten
gets me the money. . . . What next? Do you realize it means
we have to drop everything, and I have five portraits in the
works, and important letters to write, and I've left my watch
to be repaired. . . . And if we do go, then where?

VERA
If you want my opinion, you're taking it all too seriously. I
was just sitting here with Lyuba reminiscing, and we came
to the conclusion that you have absolutely nothing to fear
from Lyonya Barbashin.

TROSHCHEYKIN
Do you have to keep calling him Lyonya all the time? What
is he, some child prodigy? I know, Vishnevski tried to "calm
me down," too. I certainly put him in his place. Now there's
no longer any hope of official assistance—the toad got

offended. I'm no coward—I'm not afraid for myself, but at the same time I have no desire for some bastard to come along and put a bullet into me.

VERA

There's one little thing I don't understand, Alyosha. I distinctly recall how, not so long ago, all of us together discussed the question of what would happen when Barbashin came back.
(Lyubov' has gone out.)

TROSHCHEYKIN

Supposing we did. . . .

VERA

And on that occasion, you quite calmly—no, don't stand with your back to me.

TROSHCHEYKIN

If I am looking out the window, it is for good reason.

VERA

Are you afraid he is lying in wait for you?

TROSHCHEYKIN

Oh, I have no doubt that he is waiting somewhere nearby for the right moment. . . .

VERA

. . . At the time you calmly foresaw everything, and insisted that you didn't bear him any grudge, that one day you would be drinking to eternal friendship together. In short, you were all meekness and magnanimity.

TROSHCHEYKIN

I don't remember that. On the contrary, not a day has passed that I haven't been tormented by the thought of his return. You think I haven't been preparing to leave? But how could I foresee that they would all of a sudden pardon him? Tell me, how could I? In a couple of months I would have had my show. . . . And besides, I'm expecting certain letters. . . . In a year we could have moved away. . . . Forever, of course!
(Lyubov' returns.)

LYUBOV'

There. We're going to have lunch in a moment. You'll stay, won't you, Verochka?

VERA

No, my sweet, I'll be running along. I'll look in on Mama once more and go on home. When Vánechka comes home for lunch from the hospital, I must be there to feed him, you know. I'll be back this afternoon.

LYUBOV'

Whatever you say.

VERA

By the way, that quarrel of his with Mama is beginning to irritate me. Imagine getting offended at an old woman because she dared to gossip that he had given somebody a wrong diagnosis. It's awfully silly.

LYUBOV'

Be sure to come right after lunch.

TROSHCHEYKIN

Listen, you two, this is sheer insanity! I'm telling you for the last time, Lyuba — today's festival must be cancelled. To hell with it!

LYUBOV'
(to Vera)
Funny man, isn't he? He'll go on nagging like this for another hour without tiring one bit.

TROSHCHEYKIN
Splendid. Only I do not intend to be present.

LYUBOV'
You know, Verochka, I think I'll walk you to the corner — the sun's out.

TROSHCHEYKIN
You're going out into the street? You —

VERA
Take pity on your husband, Lyúbinka. There'll be time enough for walks.

TROSHCHEYKIN
Oh no, my friend. . . . If you . . . if you do such a thing. . . .

LYUBOV'
All right, all right, just stop yelling.

VERA
Well, I'm off. So you like my gloves? Cute, aren't they? And you calm down, Alyosha. . . . Get a grip on yourself. . . . There's nobody thirsting for your blood. . . .

TROSHCHEYKIN
I envy your equanimity, dove! Wait till your sister gets

bumped off, then you'll remember, and have a fit. I'm leaving tomorrow in any case. And if I don't get the money, I'll know they want my ruin. Oh, if only I were a loan shark or a grocer, how they would look after my safety! No matter, no matter. Some day my paintings will make people scratch their heads, only I won't see that day. How vile! A murderer roams under your windows at night, and the only advice a fat lawyer can give you is to let things settle down. I'd like to know who is going to do the settling down! Is it I who am supposed to settle down while bumping along the cobblestones in my coffin? No, siree—I'm very sorry! I still intend to stand up for my rights!

VERA

Good-by, Lyubinka. So, I'll be back soon. Surely everything will be all right, won't it? Still, perhaps you'd better stay home today.

TROSHCHEYKIN

Lyuba! Hurry, it's him!

VERA

Oh, I want to have a look, too.

TROSHCHEYKIN

Over there!

LYUBOV'

Where? I don't see anything.

TROSHCHEYKIN

There, by the newsstand. There, there, there. Standing right by it. Can't you see?

LYUBOV'
Which one? By the curb? With the paper?

TROSHCHEYKIN
Yes, yes, yes!
(Antonina Pavlovna comes in.)

ANTONINA PAVLOVNA
Marfa is already serving lunch, children.

TROSHCHEYKIN
Now are you satisfied? So, who was right? Don't stick your head out! Are you crazy? . . .

CURTAIN

ACT TWO

The living room, which also serves as dining room. Lyubov', Antonina Pavlovna. Table, sideboard. Marfa, a ruddy-faced old woman with two meaty growths on her temple and near her nose, is clearing away the remains of lunch, and the tablecloth.

MARFA
What time is he coming, Lyubov' Ivanovna?

LYUBOV'
He's not coming at all. Your solicitude can be preserved for another day.

MARFA
What stewed preserves? I didn't make any stewed —

LYUBOV'
Never mind. The *embroidered* tablecloth, please.

MARFA
What a fright Mr. Alex gave me! The man will be wearing glasses, he says.

LYUBOV'
Glasses? What kind of piffle is that?

MARFA
It's all the same to me. Never laid eyes on him in my life.

ANTONINA PAVLOVNA
Bravo! He's certainly coached her to perfection.

LYUBOV'
I never doubted for a minute that Alyosha would drive her batty. When he begins giving physical descriptions of people, then it's either untrue or tendentious. *(to Marfa)* Did they deliver everything from the pastry shop?

MARFA
What you ordered they delivered. Pale, he says, turned-up collar, he says, and how am I to tell a pale face from a red one, with the collar up and the dark glasses?
(She goes out.)

LYUBOV'
Acting the part of a silly harridan.

ANTONINA PAVLOVNA
You'd better ask Ryovshin to keep an eye on her or else she won't let in anyone at all in her fright.

LYUBOV'
Point is, she's lying. She can tell the difference perfectly well when she wants to. After all this crazy talk I, too, am beginning to believe he'll suddenly show up.

ANTONINA PAVLOVNA

Poor Alyosha! That's who I'm sorry for. . . . He frightened *her* out of her wits, then gave *me* a tongue-lashing for no reason at all. . . . Whatever did I say at lunch to deserve it?

LYUBOV'

Well, you can understand his being upset. *(a short pause)* He's even beginning to hallucinate. . . . To mistake some blond shorty, peacefully buying his paper, for—It's *ridiculous.* But you can't talk him out of it. He's decided that Barbashin is lurking beneath our windows, therefore, it has to be so.

ANTONINA PAVLOVNA

I just thought of something funny: all of this would make a terrific play.

LYUBOV'

Dear, dear Mama! You'd be perfect for the part of the jolly, plump lady. I'm so happy that fate gave me a literary mother. Someone else would be wailing and complaining in your place, and you are creating.

ANTONINA PAVLOVNA

But it's true. It could be transferred to the stage with hardly any changes, only a little condensing. The first act would be a morning, such as we had today. . . . Of course I would replace Ryovshin by some other, less trivial messenger. For example, a comic, red-nosed policeman or a lawyer with a speech impediment.[4] Or else some femme fatale whom Barbashin had abandoned

---

[4] "Speech impediment" has been substituted for "Jewish accent" so that those unfamiliar with Nabokov's lifelong contempt for anti-Semitism might not get the impression that he shared his character's vulgarity.

long ago. It could be whipped up with no trouble at all. And then it would start to develop.

LYUBOV'

In a word: "Gentlemen, Gogol's Inspector General has arrived in our town." I see you consider this whole business an additional birthday surprise. Good for you, Mummy! Tell me, how would you say it will develop? Will there be any shooting?

ANTONINA PAVLOVNA

Oh, I still have to think that out. Perhaps he will commit suicide at your feet.

LYUBOV'

I'd like so much to know the ending. Chekhov said that if there is a rifle hanging on the wall in the first act of a play, it was sure to be fired in the last, but Leonid Victorovich used to say it was bound to misfire.

ANTONINA PAVLOVNA

Please, just don't do anything rash. Think, Lyubushka, how *lucky* you are not to have married him. And how cross you used to get with me when, from the very first, I tried to reason with you!

LYUBOV'

Mummy, dear, you'd better stick to your play. Our recollections never get along together, so there's no point in having them meet. Say, didn't you want to read us your story?

ANTONINA PAVLOVNA

I'll read it when the guests get here. Have a little patience. I rounded it out and polished it before lunch. *(a short pause)* I can't understand why I didn't get a letter from Misha. Strange. Could he be sick? ...

LYUBOV'

Nonsense. He forgot, and at the last minute will gallop off to the telegraph office.

(Ryovshin enters, in what appears to be a cutaway.)

RYOVSHIN

Hello again. How's the old morale?

LYUBOV'

Splendid. Are you off to a funeral or something?

RYOVSHIN

Why? Because of the black suit? What is one supposed to wear for a family celebration, for the fiftieth birthday of our beloved authoress? I believe you like chrysanthemums, Antonina Pavlovna. ... They're the most literary of flowers for the most literary of mothers.

ANTONINA PAVLOVNA

How lovely! Thank you, my dear. Lyubushka, there's a vase over there.

RYOVSHIN

And you know why? Because in every chrysanthemum there's a theme and a mum.

LYUBOV'

Life of the party. ...

RYOVSHIN

And where is Alexey Maximovich?

ANTONINA PAVLOVNA

The poor dear is working on his portrait of the jeweler's boy. Well, do you have any news? Any more encounters with the escapee?

LYUBOV'

I knew it: now the rumor will start going around that he's an escaped convict.

RYOVSHIN

No news of any importance. How do you assess the situation, Antonina Pavlovna?

ANTONINA PAVLOVNA

Optimistically. By the way, I'm convinced that if I could talk to him for five minutes everything would get cleared up.

LYUBOV'

No, this vase won't do. It's too low.

ANTONINA PAVLOVNA

He is a brute, and I know how to talk to brutes. A patient of my late husband's was once about to inflict bodily harm on him, because his wife had supposedly not been saved in time. I subdued him in a wink. Here, give me those flowers. I'll take care of them myself—I have plenty of vases. He cooled down immediately.

LYUBOV'

Mummy, that never happened.

ANTONINA PAVLOVNA

Of course not. Whenever I have an amusing story to tell, it's always got to be an invention of mine. *(leaves with flowers)*

RYOVSHIN
Ah, such is the fate of all authors.

LYUBOV'
Sure there's nothing new? Or did you do some more amateur sleuthing anyway?

RYOVSHIN
Why are you being belligerent toward me again? My love. . . . I mean, my dear. . . . You know that I only —

LYUBOV'
I know that you only adore meddling in other people's business like a hick-town Sherlock Holmes.

RYOVSHIN
Come on, what are you saying? . . .

LYUBOV'
Then, swear that you didn't see him again.
(very loud noise of shattering glass. Troshcheykin runs in.)

TROSHCHEYKIN
The mirror is broken! That rotten kid smashed the *mirror* with a ball!

LYUBOV'
Where? Which one?

TROSHCHEYKIN
The one in the front hall. Go on, go on, take a look—it's a lovely sight.

LYUBOV'
I told you to send him right home after the sitting, so he wouldn't turn the place into a soccer field. Of course, he goes crazy with those five balls around. . . . *(goes out quickly)*

TROSHCHEYKIN
They say it's a terrible omen. I don't believe in omens, but for some reason, in my life they have always come true. How unpleasant. . . . Well, let's hear the news.

RYOVSHIN
Yes, I do have a little something for you. But I emphatically request that you not breathe a word to your wife. It'll only alarm her, especially since she considers the entire matter a personal affair of hers.

TROSHCHEYKIN
Okay, okay. . . . Out with it.

RYOVSHIN
Well—as soon as I left you I headed for his street and began my watch.

TROSHCHEYKIN
Did you see him? Did you speak with him?

RYOVSHIN
Wait. Let me proceed in orderly fashion.

TROSHCHEYKIN
To hell with orderly fashion!

RYOVSHIN
An anarchist remark to say the least, but hold on for a

minute anyway. Today you already ruined things with Vishnevski by that way of yours of going off half-cocked.

TROSHCHEYKIN

Oh, that—to hell with it. I'll make other arrangements.

RYOVSHIN

It was, as you know, close to ten. At exactly ten-thirty Arshinski enters the building—you know whom I mean?

TROSHCHEYKIN

No wonder I saw him on the boulevard—that's where he must have been heading.

RYOVSHIN

I decided to wait in spite of the drizzle. Fifteen minutes go by, then thirty, then forty. "Well," I say, "he probably won't come out until night."

TROSHCHEYKIN

To whom?

RYOVSHIN

What do you mean to whom?

TROSHCHEYKIN

To whom did you say that?

RYOVSHIN

Oh, there was a very sensible salesman there from one of the stores, and there was also a lady from the house next door standing with us. A couple of other people—I don't recall who they were. It's totally unimportant. In short, the consensus was that he had already been out for cigarettes in the morning, and probably would be going out very soon for lunch. At this point the weather improved somewhat. . . .

TROSHCHEYKIN
I implore you—skip the descriptions of nature. Did you see him or not?

RYOVSHIN
I did. At eleven-forty he went out with Arshinski.

TROSHCHEYKIN
Aha!

RYOVSHIN
Dressed in a light-gray suit, shaven clean as a god, but with a ghastly expression: black eyes burning, a smirk on his lips, brows knit in a frown. He took leave of Arshinski at the corner and went into the restaurant. I saunter by, inconspicuously as it were, and what do I see? There he is sitting at a table by the window, jotting something down in a little notebook. At that moment his appetizer arrived and he got busy with that. Well, I realized I was a mortal too, and decided to go home and have lunch.

TROSHCHEYKIN
So he looked glum?

RYOVSHIN
Glum as hell.

TROSHCHEYKIN
If I were making the laws, an expression like that would be enough to drag somebody off to the police station, and pronto. Is that all?

RYOVSHIN

Patience. Before I had a chance to take five steps, a waiter from the restaurant overtakes me with a note. From him. Here it is. See, it's folded, and on the outside, in his hand, it says "To Mr. Ryovshin, personal." Try and guess what it said.

TROSHCHEYKIN

Hurry up! Hand it over. There's no time for guessing.

RYOVSHIN

Come on, take a guess.

TROSHCHEYKIN

Give it to me, I tell you.

RYOVSHIN

You wouldn't have guessed anyway. Here.

TROSHCHEYKIN

I don't understand. . . . There's nothing written here . . . a blank piece of paper.

RYOVSHIN

That's the eerie part of it. That white paper is more terrifying than any threat. It virtually blinded me.

TROSHCHEYKIN

He's not without talent, the scoundrel. Anyway, it must be preserved. Might come in handy as evidence. No, I can't go on living like this. . . . What time is it?

RYOVSHIN

Three-twenty-five.

TROSHCHEYKIN

In half an hour that obnoxious Vagabundov woman will be here: you can imagine, can't you, how much I feel like painting portraits today? And this waiting. . . . I'm expecting a phone call tonight. . . . If the money doesn't come through, you'll have to go find me a straitjacket. What a horrible situation! I've taken advance payments all around, and there's not a red cent in the house! Can't you think of *something?*

RYOVSHIN

Well, maybe I can. . . . Actually I don't have any extra cash at the moment myself, but if worst came to worst I could get you enough for a ticket—for somewhere nearby, of course—and for a stay of, say, two weeks, but under the condition that you let Lyubov' Ivanovna go to my sister's place in the country. After that we'll see.

TROSHCHEYKIN

Oh, no, nothing doing. I can't go without her, you know that perfectly well. I'm like a little child. I'm totally incompetent, I botch everything.

RYOVSHIN

Can't help it—you'll just have to go ahead and botch. She'll be very happy there—my sister is first-rate, and I'll look in from time to time myself. Keep in mind, Alexey Maximovich, that when the target is divided into two parts, and those parts are in two different places, there's nothing left to shoot at.

TROSHCHEYKIN

Oh, I don't dispute that. . . . On the whole it seems like a good idea. . . . Only Lyuba will balk at it.

RYOVSHIN

We'll convince her somehow. Just present it as your idea and not mine. It'll be more proper that way. We are now speaking as one gentleman to another, and I venture to assume that you are perfectly aware of the situation.

TROSHCHEYKIN

We'll see, we'll see. Now tell me, sir: if I were really to leave tomorrow, should I perhaps wear makeup? I happen to have a beard and wig left over from our theatre group. What do you think?

RYOVSHIN

Why not? Go ahead, but just don't frighten the other passengers.

TROSHCHEYKIN

Yes, all this is somehow. . . . On the other hand, though, I think that since he has promised, he'll get it for me, right?

RYOVSHIN

Alexey Maximovich, how do *I* know how good your credit is? *(Lyubov' and Vera enter.)*

VERA
(to Ryovshin)
Hello, Mr. Confidant.

TROSHCHEYKIN

Here, Lyuba, listen to what he has to say. . . . *(digs into his pocket for the note)*

RYOVSHIN

My friend, you agreed not to tell that risqué joke to the ladies.

LYUBOV'
No, let's hear it immediately.

TROSHCHEYKIN
Oh, leave me alone, all of you! *(goes out)*

LYUBOV'
(to Ryovshin)
Nice going!

RYOVSHIN
I swear to you, Lyubov' Ivanovna. . . .

LYUBOV'
Here's what I'd like you to do for me. There's the most ungodly
mess in the front hall. Look, I just cut my finger on some glass.
Go see what you can do — you'll have to bring the other mirror
from the bedroom. Marfa can't do it.

RYOVSHIN
With pleasure.

LYUBOV'
And then you'll keep an eye out so she doesn't shoo away
some innocent guest whom she has mistaken for the person
to whom you talked this afternoon.

RYOVSHIN
Lyubov' Ivanovna, I didn't talk to him, I swear to God.

LYUBOV'
And while you're at it, tell her to come and help me
set the table for tea. They'll start arriving in a minute.

VERA

Please let me do it, Lyubochka. I adore doing it.

RYOVSHIN

You'll see—I'll be a regular Cerberus. *(goes out)*

LYUBOV'

For some reason, every time I'm expecting guests, I think about how I've frittered away my life. No, better use the little ones. . . . So you were saying he has the same housekeeper as before?

VERA

Yes, he does. These?

LYUBOV'

They'll do fine. And how does Lisa know her?

VERA

She once recommended Lisa to the Stanislavskis, and I got Lisa from them. Well, when I came home from your house today, I found her in the middle of an animated conversation with the janitor. Barbashin this, Barbashin that—she couldn't stop babbling. Anyway, it seems he arrived yesterday without warning, about seven p.m., but everything was in perfect order, as the housekeeper had lived there all this time.

LYUBOV'

Yes, I remember the apartment well.

VERA

Last night he went out somewhere, and today he spent

practically the whole day typing letters.

LYUBOV'
Vera, Vera, how trivial all this is. Why should I pay any attention to the prattle of two old gossips?

VERA
Still, you've got to admit it's interesting! And a little frightening.

LYUBOV'
Yes—a little frightening. . . .
(Enter Marfa with the cake and Antonina Pavlovna with the fruit.)

VERA
Suppose he's really planning something sinister? Oh, yes—there's something else: it seems he lost a lot of weight in prison, and the first thing he did was order pork chops and a bottle of champagne. I must say Lisa felt very sorry for you. . . . About how many people are coming? Did I count right?

LYUBOV'
The Writer. . . . Aunt Zhenya and Uncle Paul. . . . Old Mrs. Nikoladze. . . . Meshaev. . . .Ryovshin. . . . the four of us. . . . I think that's all. Let's set another glass, just in case.

VERA
For whom? Do you mean. . . .

ANTONINA PAVLOVNA
Meshaev said his brother might be coming. Oh, Lyubúsha. . . .

LYUBOV'
What?

ANTONINA PAVLOVNA

No, never mind. I thought this was one of the old little forks.
(Troshcheykin comes in.)

TROSHCHEYKIN

Thank heavens, at last people are beginning to wake up.
Lyuba, Kuprikov just called, and implored us not to go out
in the street. He'll be over in a moment. Apparently there's
something new. He didn't want to tell me over the phone.

LYUBOV'

What a pity he's coming. I simply can't stand your
colleagues. See, Vera—the extra glass came in handy. Put
another one on the table, will you?

TROSHCHEYKIN

Yes, it seems people are finally beginning to understand the
situation we are in. Well, I guess I'll fortify myself a little.

LYUBOV'

Leave the cake alone; don't be a boor. At least wait until the
guests arrive, then you can stuff yourself on the sly.

TROSHCHEYKIN

Not a chance—when the guests arrive I'll be in my room. All
right, I'll just take a piece of candy.

LYUBOV'

Alyosha, don't spoil it. I arranged everything so beautifully. Look, in a moment you're going to get a slap on
the fingers.

ANTONINA PAVLOVNA

Here's a little piece of cake for you. *(The doorbell rings.)*

TROSHCHEYKIN

That must be old Mrs. Vagabundov. I'll try and finish her
today. My hands are trembling, I can't hold a brush, and
still I'm going to finish her, damn it. And I'm certainly not
going to kill myself trying to make a masterpiece out of it.

VERA

It's gluttony you are trembling with.
(Ryovshin enters.)

RYOVSHIN

There's someone at the door, but, judging from certain
characteristics, she is not part of today's program. Name of
Eleonora Shnap. Shall I invite her in?

TROSHCHEYKIN

What's the meaning of this, Antonina Pavlovna? What kind
of people do you invite? Do we kick her out?

ANTONINA PAVLOVNA

I didn't invite her. Shnap? Shnap? Oh, you know,
Lyubushka, wasn't she your midwife?

LYUBOV'

Yes. Dreadful woman. Send her away.

ANTONINA PAVLOVNA

After all, she did come to wish me a happy birthday. We can't
send her away — it wouldn't be nice.

LYUBOV'

Whatever you say. *(to Ryovshin)* What are you waiting
for? Show her in.

VERA

Last time we saw her was at the funeral. . . .

LYUBOV'

I don't remember. I don't remember anything. . . .

TROSHCHEYKIN
(about to exit left)
Count me out in any case.

VERA

You're making a mistake, Alyosha. Her first husband's niece was married to Barbashin's first cousin.

TROSHCHEYKIN

Ah! That's a different story. . . .
(Enter Eleonora Shnap. Violet dress. Pince-nez.)

ANTONINA PAVLOVNA

How kind of you to drop by. Actually I didn't want the word to get around, but apparently it did.

ELEONORA SHNAP

Alas, ze whole town speaking about it iss.

ANTONINA PAVLOVNA

Alas is right! That's well put. I know myself it's nothing to be proud of, just another step closer to the grave. Of course you know my son-in-law and Lyubov', and this is my other daughter, Vera. Their names mean Love and Faith. There isn't any Hope.

ELEONORA SHNAP
Good Gott! Alzo you mean it is hopeless?

ANTONINA PAVLOVNA
Yes, this is an absolutely hopeless family. *(laughs)*
How I would have liked to have a little green-
eyed Hope.

ELEONORA SHNAP
So? . . .

LYUBOV'
There's a misunderstanding here. Mummy!

ANTONINA PAVLOVNA
Sit down, please. We'll be having tea in a moment.

ELEONORA SHNAP
As zoon ess today I foundt oudt I shlap my hans togedder. I
to myzelf tink right avay to look in I must go.

LYUBOV'
And see how they're taking it?

ANTONINA PAVLOVNA
Very, very kind. And who was it that told you? Zhenya—I
mean Yevghenia Vasilyevna?

ELEONORA SHNAP
Nein. Madame Vishnevski.

ANTONINA PAVLOVNA
How did she know? Alyosha, have you been gossiping?

LYUBOV'

Mummy, I'm telling you there's an idiotic mix-up here. *(to Eleonora Shnap)* You see, it's my mother's birthday today.

ELEONORA SHNAP

Unhappy mudder! Now I everything untershtandt!

TROSHCHEYKIN

Tell me about him. . . . Perhaps you . . .

LYUBOV'

Stop it, please. What is this silly talk?

ELEONORA SHNAP

A friend in time of zerious trouble you recognize, an enemy in time of little troubles. Zo my professor Esser always zaid. I could not not come. . . .

VERA

Nothing terrible has happened. What are you talking about? We are all perfectly relaxed, and even in a festive mood.

ELEONORA SHNAP

Ja, it iss goot. Never let zuch tings get ze besser off you. Dass iss ze vay: holdt firm! *(to Lyubov')* My poor, poor vun! Poor fictim! Tank Gott our little baby did not liff all tiss to see!

LYUBOV'

Tell me, Eleonora Karlovna, do you have a lot of work these days? Is there a great deal of childbearing going on?

ELEONORA SHNAP

Oh, I know zat my reputation zat of a coldhearted woman doctor is, but believe zat, bezides ze forceps, in my breast zere beats a gross, sad heart.

ANTONINA PAVLOVNA
In any case, we are very touched by your sympathy.

LYUBOV'
Mama. This is unbearable. . . .
(The doorbell rings.)

TROSHCHEYKIN
Listen, just between you and me — did you by any chance see
this man today?

ELEONORA SHNAP
Chust now I look in, but he wass not there. Why, you haff a
message for him?
(Ryovshin enters.)

RYOVSHIN
Mrs. Vagabundov to see you, Alexey Maximovich.

TROSHCHEYKIN
Be right there. Listen, Lyuba — when Kuprikov comes, call
me immediately.
*(Mrs. Vagabundov enters like a bouncing ball: she is very elderly,
white dress trimmed with lace, lace fan and velvet neck ribbon,
apricot-colored hair.)*

MRS. VAGABUNDOV
Greetings, greetings, I know I intrude
But, in view of what's happened I don't think I'm rude—

TROSHCHEYKIN
Let's go, let's go!

MRS. VAGABUNDOV
— and in view of events —

LYUBOV'
Madam, he's in a great form today, you'll see!

MRS. VAGABUNDOV
There's simply no sense!
No — no — this ain't
The right time to paint.
Lord, what could be absurder
Than such a beauty to murder?

TROSHCHEYKIN
The portrait must be completed.

MRS. VAGABUNDOV
With heroics, Maestro, dispense —
I know and respect your state of suspense:
I've been widowed like you,
And not one time but two.
My conjugal bliss was a horrid deception,
And consisted without exception
Of wakes.
I see you have tea and cakes?

ANTONINA PAVLOVNA
Sit down, please do.

MRS. VAGABUNDOV
I'm thirsting for news!

TROSHCHEYKIN
Please listen to me — I'm being serious. Drink some tea, have

whatever you want—that thingum with the cream, for instance—but then I want to work on your portrait! You must realize that I'll probably be leaving tomorrow. We must finish!

ELEONORA SHNAP

So! Here is shpeaking common zense. Leave, leave and again
leave! I have always with Herr Barbashin a bit of
hail-fellow-vell-met relationship, und naturally he vill a
terrible ding do.

MRS. VAGABUNDOV

Maybe he will toss a bomb.
But does he have enough aplomb?
Yes, he might just
And, on the spot
Blow the whole lot
Of us to dust.

ANTONINA PAVLOVNA

I'm not worried for myself. There is a saying in India that
only great people die on their birthdays. The law of whole
numbers.

LYUBOV'

There's no such saying, Mummy.

MRS. VAGABUNDOV

Amazing combination,
A family fête and this revisitation!

ELEONORA SHNAP

Dass is vot I zay. And zey vere zo happy! On vot hangs the
human happiness? On a tread tin tin it hangs, zat's how ve live!

MRS. VAGABUNDOV
(to Antonina Pavlovna)
What a darling little sieve!
More water, please, that's much too strong. . . .
Yes, everything's dandy, then he comes along!

VERA
Ladies, ladies, it isn't funeral time yet. Everybody knew
perfectly well that one day Barbashin would be back, and the
fact that he is back a little early doesn't really make any
difference. I'm certain he's forgotten all about it.
(The doorbell rings.)

MRS. VAGABUNDOV
You mustn't say that. I've been through this game. . . .
Believe me, the jail term has but fanned the flame!
My dear Mr. Alex, it just isn't befitting—
Let's forget the sitting.
Holding still is a thing I can't face.
My bosom will heave and my pulse will race.
(Ryovshin comes in.)

RYOVSHIN
Yevghenia Vasilyevna and consort, and also Mr. Kuprikov,
professional artist.

TROSHCHEYKIN
Wait a minute—he's come to see me.
(Troshcheykin goes out.)

ELEONORA SHNAP
(to Mrs. Vagabundov)
I undershtandt you zo goot! My heart is bleeding alzo.

Speaking betveen me und you, now I am kvite sure the child wass hiss. . . .

MRS. VAGABUNDOV

There's absolutely no doubt!

But I'm glad a professional opinion bears me out.

(Aunt Zhenya and Uncle Paul enter. She is a buxom lady in a silk dress, and would be wearing a bonnet with ribbons if it were a half-century earlier. He wears his white hair in a crew cut and has a dashing mustache that he preens with a little brush. He is of pleasing appearance, but ga-ga.)

YEVGHENIA VASILYEVNA

Don't tell me it's all true! Did he actually run away from hard labor, and try to break in here last night?

VERA

That's ridiculous, Aunt Zhenya. Why do you listen to such clap-trap?

YEVGHENIA VASILYEVNA

Clap-trap my eye! Today Uncle Paul himself. . . . Here, let him tell you. He described it beautifully to me. You'll hear for yourself. *(to Antonina Pavlovna)* Happy birthday, Antonina, even though it's hardly a day for congratulations. *(to Lyubov', indicating Eleonora Shnap)* I'm not on speaking terms with that bitch. If I'd known, I wouldn't have come. . . . Paul, everybody is waiting.

UNCLE PAUL

The other day . . .

AUNT ZHENYA

No, no—today.

UNCLE PAUL

Today, as I was saying, quite unexpectedly, I suddenly saw a certain party coming out of a restaurant.

MRS. VAGABUNDOV

Out of a restaurant, you say?
So early in the day?
How much liquor had he put away?

ANTONINA PAVLOVNA

Oh, Zhénichka, why do you spoil me like this? They're lovely! Lyubochka, just look at these handkerchiefs.

ELEONORA SHNAP

Ja. Zey vill be goot to cry into.

UNCLE PAUL

Making allowance for the brevity of my observation and the rapidity of the subject's motion, I affirm that I was in a sober state.

AUNT ZHENYA

No, not you . . . him.

UNCLE PAUL

Very well, him.

VERA

Uncle Paul, you're imagining things. It's not a dangerous symptom, but it ought to be watched.

LYUBOV'

Anyway, all this isn't very interesting. . . . What may I give you? Would you like some cake first? Mama is going to read us her new fairy tale now.

UNCLE PAUL
This is my firm conviction, and it won't change even under
threat of conviction.

AUNT ZHENYA
Go on, go on, Paul. . . . Now you're getting warmed up.

UNCLE PAUL
He was walking, I was walking. And the other day I saw a
woman get hurt falling off a bicycle.

MRS. VAGABUNDOV
What disaster, what dismay!
It's time to leave, that's clear as day!
Every one, for heaven's sake! . . .
I think I'll have a little more cake.

ANTONINA PAVLOVNA
Lyuba, dear, shouldn't we wait until everybody is here?

LYUBOV'
No, it doesn't matter—please begin.

ANTONINA PAVLOVNA
All right. Here we go. So, this fairy tale, or rather sketch,
concludes my *Illumined Lakes* cycle. Paul, dear, will you sit
down please?

UNCLE PAUL
I would rather stand.
(The doorbell rings.)

AUNT ZHENYA

I don't understand it. He told it so colorfully, so nicely, before, and now something has jammed. Maybe he'll get going again later on. *(to her husband)* You worry me lately.
(Ryovshin enters, ushering in Mrs. Nikoladze, a wizened little old lady with short-trimmed hair, dressed in black, and the Famous Writer. He is old, used to being lionized, and speaks slowly, weightily, a little nasally, with throat-clearing noises that give his words impressive emphasis. He is wearing a dinner jacket.)

ANTONINA PAVLOVNA

Ah, at last!

WRITER

Well. . . . It appears one is supposed to wish you a happy birthday.

ANTONINA PAVLOVNA

I'm so glad to see you here in my house! I kept worrying you might rush off somewhere, bird of passage that you are.

WRITER

I don't think I know anyone here. . . .

MRS. NIKOLADZE

Happy birthday. Some candy. Only a trifle.

ANTONINA PAVLOVNA

Thank you, darling. You shouldn't have gone to the expense for my sake!

WRITER
(to Vera)

Haven't we met somewhere before, my dear?

VERA
At His Highness's reception, right, dear sir?

WRITER
At His Highness's reception. . . . Ah, bravo. I see you're a tease.

LYUBOV'
What can I offer you?

WRITER
What can you offer me. . . . Mm—yes. What's that you have there—one of those things people eat after funerals? Oh, it's a fruitcake. Very similar. I thought you were holding a wake.

LYUBOV'
I have no reason to hold a wake, Pyotr Nikolaevich.

WRITER
Oh, really? Well, I don't know, my dear. The mood is pretty indigo here. The only one missing is the reverend.

LYUBOV'
What will you have? Some of this?

WRITER
No, I am an antidulcinist, an enemy of all things sweet. How about some liquor?

ANTONINA PAVLOVNA
In a minute we'll have the Moët, Pyotr Nikolaevich.

Lyubushka, ask Ryovshin to open the bottle.

WRITER

How come you have Moët? You must be getting richer and richer.

LYUBOV'

If you must know, the wine merchant gave it to my husband in payment for a head-and-shoulders portrait.

WRITER

Great thing, to be a portrait artist. You develop horns. Of plenty, that is. Say, would you have a little brandy for me?

LYUBOV'

You'll be served right away.

MRS. VAGABUNDOV

Pyotr Nikolaevich, pardon a widow's confession. . . .
To meet you in person makes such an impression!
I'm so honored I could die.
Not only I,
But everyone loves your creations.

WRITER

Thank you.

MRS. VAGABUNDOV

But do give us your evaluation
Of the situation.

WRITER

Of what situation, Madam?

MRS. VAGABUNDOV
You mean you haven't yet learned
Who has unexpectedly returned?

ANTONINA PAVLOVNA
(taking the snifter out of Marfa's hands)
There you are.

WRITER
I have been informed. *(to Lyubov')* Tell me, my dear, are your
knees shaking? Let's have a look. . . . In my youth I once fell
in love with a girl just because of her knees.

LYUBOV'
I'm not afraid of anything, Pyotr Nikolaevich.

WRITER
You *are* fearless, aren't you? M-mm—this assassin is quite a
connoisseur.

MRS. NIKOLADZE
What's that? I don't understand anything. What masseur?
What assassin? What happened?

WRITER
To your health, my dear. Your brandy is nothing to brag
about, I must say.

ELEONORA SHNAP
(to Mrs. Nikoladze)
I zee you know nussing about itt. I'll tell you.

MRS. VAGABUNDOV
If you'll allow,

It's my turn now.

ELEONORA SHNAP
No, it's mine. Please not to interfere.

LYUBOV'
Mummy — now, please. . . .

ANTONINA PAVLOVNA
When you came in, Pyotr Nikolaevich, I was going to read
them a little piece of mine, but now, in front of you, I feel
kind of abashed.

WRITER
Stop the pretense. You'll enjoy it even more. I assume that in
your youth you prattled between kisses like all deceitful
women.

ANTONINA PAVLOVNA
I have long since forgotten such things, Pyotr Nikolaevich.

WRITER
Go ahead. Let's hear it.

ANTONINA PAVLOVNA
The title is "The Resurrection of the Swan."

WRITER
"The Resurrection of the Swan.". . . The death of Lazarus. . . .
The second and final death. . . . Not bad. . . .

ANTONINA PAVLOVNA
No, Pyotr Nikolaevich, not Lazarus — the swan.

WRITER
Forgive me. I was talking to myself. Something flashed through my mind. A reflex of the imagination.

TROSHCHEYKIN
(appearing at the door)
Lyuba, come here for a minute.

LYUBOV'
You come here, Alyosha.

TROSHCHEYKIN
Lyuba!

LYUBOV'
Come here. Mr. Kuprikov will also find this interesting.

TROSHCHEYKIN
Suit yourself.
(comes into the room with Kuprikov and the Reporter. Kuprikov is a tritely picturesque picture-painter, in a jacket with padded shoulders, an extremely dark shirt and an extremely light necktie. The Reporter is a young man with parted hair and a fountain pen.)

TROSHCHEYKIN
This is Igor Olegovich Kuprikov. Get acquainted. And this gentleman has come to interview us for the *Sun.*

KUPRIKOV
(to Lyubov')
Honored to meet you. . . . I've given your husband all my information.

MRS. VAGABUNDOV

Oh, I'm filled with expectation!
Let's hear your information.

AUNT ZHENYA

Now, Paul! Now is your chance to shine! You told it so beautifully before. Paul! Come on. . . . Mr. Kuprikov, Alyosha — my husband, here, also saw . . .

UNCLE PAUL

Be glad to. It happened like this. The ambulance was coming around the corner from the left, and the lady on the bicycle was coming full speed from the right — a rather fat lady, with a red beret, as far as I could make out.

WRITER

Halt. You've lost the floor. Next.

VERA

Come, Uncle Paul, come, my sweet. I'll give you a piece of candy.

AUNT ZHENYA

I don't understand what is the matter. . . . He's developed some kind of mechanical defect.

KUPRIKOV
(to the Writer)
May I?

WRITER

Maestro Kuprikov has the floor.

LYUBOV'
(to her husband)

I don't know why all this has to be transformed into some kind of nightmarish farce. Why did you bring this reporter with his note pad? Mama is about to read her story. Please, let's not talk about Barbashin anymore.

TROSHCHEYKIN
What can I do? . . . Leave me in peace. I'm dying a slow death. *(to the guests)* What time is it? Does anybody have a watch?
(All look at their watches.)

WRITER
Five on the dot. We are listening, Mr. Kuprikov.

KUPRIKOV
I have just been reporting the following fact to Alexey Maximovich. I shall now give a short version. As I was walking today at two-thirty through the city park, namely along the avenue that ends at the urn, I saw Leonid Barbashin sitting on a green bench.

WRITER
You don't say?

KUPRIKOV
He was sitting motionless, pondering something. The shadows of the foliage lay in beautiful patterns around his yellow shoes.

WRITER
Fine . . . bravo. . . .

KUPRIKOV
He did not see me, and I observed him for some time from

behind a thick tree trunk, on which some person had carved some initials, which, however, were already blackened with age. Barbashin was gazing at the ground and thinking weighty thoughts. Then he shifted his position and began looking to one side at a bit of sunbathed lawn. After about twenty minutes he got up and left. The first yellow leaf of the season fell onto the empty bench.

WRITER

A vital and beautifully phrased report. Does anyone wish to comment?

KUPRIKOV

From which I concluded that he was planning some evil deed and therefore I once again address to you, Lyubov' Ivanovna, and to you, dear Alyosha, in the presence of witnesses, an emphatic appeal that you take maximum precautions.

TROSHCHEYKIN

Yes! But *what* precautions? *What* precautions?

WRITER

That, as Shakespeare would have said, is the question. *(to the Reporter)* And what do you have to say, my dear *Sun*?

REPORTER

I'd like to ask Mrs. Troshcheykin a few questions. May I?

LYUBOV'

Have a cup of tea instead. Or a brandy?

REPORTER

My humble thanks. I wanted to ask you for a general

description of your emotions when you found out.

WRITER

Quite useless, dear chap. She won't tell you a single thing. Keeps silent but burns you up with her gaze. I confess that such women make me tremble with desire. As for this brandy—well, I advise against it.

ANTONINA PAVLOVNA

I'll start now if I may. . . .

WRITER

(to Reporter)

By the way, your paper has again started printing all kinds of cheap trash about me. I haven't been preparing a story based on gypsy life and would never prepare one. Shame on you.

ANTONINA PAVLOVNA

Pyotr Nikolaevich, may I?

WRITER

By all means. Attention, everybody.

ANTONINA PAVLOVNA

The first rays of the sun. . . . Oh yes, I forgot to tell you, Pyotr Nikolaevich. This is from my *Illumined Lakes* cycle. Maybe you have read some of it. . . . "The first rays of the sun playing and, as it were, frolicking, ran in a tentative chromatic scale across the smooth surface of the lake, touched the keys of the reeds, and paused amid the dark-green sedge. On this sedge, with one wing folded and the other"—
(Ryovshin comes in with Meshaev One: a ruddy blond fellow with a bouquet of similarly ruddy roses.)

RYOVSHIN

Here, Lyubov' Ivanovna, I think this is the last one. I'm tired. . . . May I have some —

LYUBOV'

Sh-sh! . . . Sit down, Osip Mikheyevich. Mama is reading her fairy tale.

MESHAEV ONE

May I interrupt the reading for just one second? I have sensational news.

SEVERAL VOICES

What happened? Tell us! How interesting!

MESHAEV ONE

Lyubov' Ivanovna! Alexey Maximovich! Know who got home from jail? Last night? Barbashin!
(general laughter)

WRITER

Is that all? My dear fellow, they even know about it in the maternity wards by now. Ye-es — Came barbashing in a little late, didn't you?

MESHAEV ONE

In that case I shall limit myself to wishing you a happy birthday, Antonina Pavlovna. *(takes out crib notes)* My wish to you is that you may entertain us for a long time to come with your splendid female talent. The days go by, but books — books, Antonina Pavlovna — remain on their shelves, and the grand cause that you selflessly serve is truly grand and abundant, and every one of your lines rings on and on in our minds and hearts in an eternal refrain. How beautiful, how fresh the roses were.[5] *(gives her the roses) (applause)*

ANTONINA PAVLOVNA

Thank you for the kind wishes, my dear Osip Mikheyevich. But why are you alone? Didn't you promise to bring your brother who lives in the country?

MESHAEV ONE

I thought he'd be here already. He probably missed his train and will come on the evening one. It's a pity: I particularly wanted to entertain all of you with our striking resemblance. But please go on with your reading!

WRITER

Yes, please. Make yourselves comfortable, ladies and gentlemen. We are probably in for a long session. Closer, closer together.
(They all move slightly upstage.)

ANTONINA PAVLOVNA

"On this sedge, with one wing folded, and the other spread wide, lay a dead swan. Its eyes were half-open, and tears still glistened on the long lashes. Meanwhile the east was coming aglow, and the sun's chords rang ever more brightly on the broad lake. With each touch of the long rays, with every light breath of air, the leaves. . . ."
(As she reads, her face remains distinct, but she seems to have receded with her armchair into the distance, so that her voice grows inaudible even though her lips continue to move and her hand keeps on turning the pages. The listeners around her, who have also lost all contact with the front of the stage, sit in motionless, drowsy attitudes: Ryovshin has frozen with a bottle of champagne between

---

[5] From Turgenev's *Prose Poems.*

his knees; the Writer's eyes are shaded by his hand. Actually, a scrim ought to descend, or a drop on which the whole group is depicted with all their attitudes exactly reproduced.)

(Troshcheykin and Lyubov' advance quickly to the proscenium.)

LYUBOV'
Alyosha, I can't stand it any longer.

TROSHCHEYKIN
I can't either. . . .

LYUBOV'
The most terrible day of our lives —

TROSHCHEYKIN
. . . our last day —

LYUBOV'
. . . has turned into a grotesque farce. From these painted specters we can expect neither salvation nor compassion.

TROSHCHEYKIN
We must run . . .

LYUBOV'
Yes, oh yes!

TROSHCHEYKIN
. . . Run — and for some reason we dawdle like motionless operatic characters singing of escape under immobile palm trees. I can sense the approaching —

LYUBOV'
. . . Danger. But what kind of danger? Oh, if only you could understand!

TROSHCHEYKIN
. . . Danger just as real as our hands, our shoulders, our cheeks. Lyuba, we are absolutely alone.

LYUBOV'
Yes, alone. But these are two solitudes, and each is a closed circle. Try to understand me!

TROSHCHEYKIN
. . . Alone on this narrow, lighted stage. Behind us, the old theatrical frippery of our whole life, the frozen masks of a second-rate comedy, and in front a dark chasm full of eyes, eyes, eyes watching us, awaiting our destruction.

LYUBOV'
Answer quick: you know that I deceive you?

TROSHCHEYKIN
Yes. But you will never leave me.

LYUBOV'
I'm so overcome with regret sometimes. Things weren't always like this.

TROSHCHEYKIN
Don't let go, Lyuba!

LYUBOV'
Our little son broke the mirror with a ball today. Hold me, Alyosha. Don't loosen your grip.

TROSHCHEYKIN

I can't see clearly. . . . Everything is growing hazy again. I don't feel you anymore. You are merging with life again. We are sinking again. Lyuba, it's all over!

LYUBOV'

Onegin, I was younger then, I was, I daresay, better-looking.[6] . . . Yes, I've weakened too. I can't remember. . . . How marvelous it was on those momentary heights.

TROSHCHEYKIN

Fantasies. Delusions. If somebody doesn't get me money today I won't live through the night.

LYUBOV'

Look, how strange: Marfa is tiptoeing toward us from the door. Look at the awful expression on her face. Just look! She's creeping in with some terrible news. She can barely move. . . .

TROSHCHEYKIN

(to Marfa)

Is it him? Out with it: is he here?

LYUBOV'

(clapping her hands and laughing)

She's nodding. Alyoshen'ka, she's nodding!

(Shchel' enters. He is round-shouldered and wears dark glasses.)

SHCHEL'

I beg your pardon. . . . My name is Ivan Ivanovich Shchel'. Your

---

[6]A. Pushkin, *Eugene Onegin*, tr. Vladimir Nabokov. Bollingen, 1964; revised ed., Princeton University Press, 1975.

half-witted maid didn't want to let me in. You don't know me, but you may know that I have a gun store across from the cathedral.

TROSHCHEYKIN
I'm listening.

SHCHEL'
I felt it my duty to come and see you. I must warn you about something.

TROSHCHEYKIN
Come closer, come closer. Here, kitty, kitty.

SHCHEL'
But you are not alone. This is a gathering. . . .

TROSHCHEYKIN
Don't pay any attention. . . . It's a kind of mirage. They are extras. They don't exist. Actually, I daubed it all myself. A poor painting, but innocuous.

SHCHEL'
Don't try to fool me. That man over there bought a shotgun from me last year.

LYUBOV'
You're imagining things. Believe us! We know better. My husband painted it in very natural colors. We are alone. You may speak freely.

SHCHEL'
In that case allow me to inform you. . . . Immediately upon learning who has returned, I recollected with alarm that at

noon today a Browning-type automatic was purchased in my store.

(The drop rises, and the reader's voice loudly concludes: ". . . and then the swan came back to life." Ryovshin uncorks the champagne. The sound of animation is immediately cut short, however.)

TROSHCHEYKIN
Did Barbashin buy it?

SHCHEL'
No, the buyer was a Mr. Arshinski. However, I can see that you understand for whom the weapon was intended.

CURTAIN

ACT THREE

*The studio again. The balls in the picture have all been painted in.
Lyubov' is alone. She looks out the window, then slowly draws the
blind. On the table lies a pack of cigarettes that Ryovshin forgot that
morning. She lights one. Sits down. A mouse (the illusion of a
mouse), taking advantage of the stillness, emerges from a crack, and
Lyubov' follows its movements with a smile; she cautiously changes
her position, leans forward, but suddenly the mouse skitters away.
Marfa enters from the left.*

LYUBOV'
There's a little mouse here again.

MARFA
And in the kitchen there are cockroaches. It's all part of the
same thing.

LYUBOV'
What's wrong with you?

MARFA
What do you think? If you don't need anything else today,

Lyubov' Ivanovna, I'll be going.

LYUBOV'
Where are you off to?

MARFA
I'll spend the night at my brother's, and tomorrow please let me leave for good. I am afraid to remain here. I'm a feeble old woman, and this house is an unhealthy place.

LYUBOV'
That wasn't a very good performance. I'll show you how it ought to be done. "Have mercy on me. . . . I am a feeble, sickly old woman. . . . I'm all in a funk. . . . The Evil One is on the loose here. . . ." That's the way. A very common part, actually. . . . You can get the hell out of here whenever you want, for all I care.

MARFA
I'll do just that, Lyubov' Ivanovna, I'll do just that. Living with a bunch of loonies isn't for me.

LYUBOV'
Don't you think that's a pretty swinish thing to do, though? You could at least have stayed the night.

MARFA
Swinish? Had my fill of swinery. Boyfriend here, boyfriend there. . . .

LYUBOV'
Oh no—not like that at all: More tremolo, more indignation. Something about Jezebel.

MARFA

I am afraid of you, Lyubov' Ivanovna. You ought to call a doctor.

LYUBOV'

A *healer*, not a doctor. No, I'm definitely not pleased with your acting. I was going to recommend you for the part of a cantankerous biddy, but now I see I can't.

MARFA

I don't need to be mended by you.

LYUBOV'

Better, better. That's enough, though. Good-by.

MARFA

Killers all over the place. 'Tis a night of ill omens.

LYUBOV'

Good-by!

MARFA

I'm going, I'm going. And tomorrow you'll pay me for the last two months. *(leaves)*

LYUBOV'

Onegin, I was younger then. . . . I was, I daresay, better-looking. . . . What a nasty old woman! Have you ever seen anything like it? Oh, what a. . . .
(Troshcheykin comes in from the right.)

TROSHCHEYKIN

Lyuba, it's all over! Baumgarten just called — there won't be any money.

LYUBOV'

I beg you. . . . Don't get so excited all the time. This tension is unbearable.

TROSHCHEYKIN

He promised to have it for me in a week. Who needs it then? What for? To hand out tips in the afterworld?

LYUBOV'

Please, Alyosha. . . . I have a splitting headache.

TROSHCHEYKIN

All right. But what do we do now? What?

LYUBOV'

It's eight-thirty now. In an hour we'll go to bed. That's all. I'm so worn out from today's bedlam that my teeth are chattering.

TROSHCHEYKIN

I beg your pardon. I'm going to have one more visitor tonight. Did you really think I was going to leave it at that? Until I am certain that no one is going to come charging in here tonight, I'm not going to bed. No siree!

LYUBOV'

And I am. And to sleep. And that is that.

TROSHCHEYKIN

Only now do I realize how destitute, how helpless we are. Somehow our life went on and our poverty went unnoticed. Listen, Lyuba: the way things are going, the only solution is to accept Ryovshin's proposal.

LYUBOV'
What do you mean, Ryovshin's proposal?

TROSHCHEYKIN
My proposal, actually. You see, he will give me money for the trip and so forth, and you will temporarily move in with his sister in the country.

LYUBOV'
A splendid plan.

TROSHCHEYKIN
Of course it's splendid. I can see no other solution to the problem. Tomorrow we'll be off—if we live through the night.

LYUBOV'
Alyosha, look into my eyes.

TROSHCHEYKIN
Cut it out. I consider it indispensable, if only for two weeks. We'll have a rest, we'll catch our breath.

LYUBOV'
Then let me tell you something. Not only will I never go to Ryovshin's sister's, but I won't budge from here.

TROSHCHEYKIN
Lyuba, Lyuba, Lyuba. Don't exasperate me. My nerves are out of control today. You obviously want to perish. . . . Goodness, it's practically night. Look, I never noticed—there's not a single street lamp outside our building. Look how far it is to the nearest one. If only the moon would hurry and come up.

LYUBOV'

Let me give you the glad news. Marfa has given notice. And already left.

TROSHCHEYKIN

There we are. The rats are abandoning the ship. Great. . . . Lyuba, I beg you on bended knee: let's go away tomorrow. Don't you see—this is inexorable hell. Fate itself is evicting us. All right, let's assume there will be a detective with us, but we can't send him out to the store, can we? That means tomorrow we have to start looking for a new maid, going to all kinds of trouble, asking your idiot sister to help. . . . These are headaches I can't face in the present situation. Come on, Lyubushka, come on, baby, what will it cost you? If you don't do it, Ryovshin won't give me the money—after all, it's a question of life and death, not of philistine propriety.

LYUBOV'

Tell me—have you ever asked yourself why people don't like you?

TROSHCHEYKIN

Who doesn't like me?

LYUBOV'

Nobody likes you. Not a living soul would lend you a penny. And many people simply feel a kind of revulsion for you.

TROSHCHEYKIN

What rot. On the contrary, you saw yourself how many people dropped in today, expressed interest, and offered their advice. . . .

LYUBOV'

I don't know. . . . I was watching your face while Mama was

reading her little piece, and I had a feeling I understood your thoughts, and how alone you felt. It even appeared to me that we exchanged a glance, the kind of glance we used to exchange once, long, long ago. Now it seems to me that it was all a mistake, that you felt nothing, and your thoughts merely kept going in a circle: will Baumgarten give me that wretched bit of cash for my escape or not?

TROSHCHEYKIN

What's the point of tormenting me, Lyuba?

LYUBOV'

I have no desire to torment you. I want to talk with you in earnest for once.

TROSHCHEYKIN

Thank goodness. It's high time you changed your infantile attitude toward danger.

LYUBOV'

No, it's not about *that* danger that I want to talk, but about our entire life together.

TROSHCHEYKIN

Oh, no. Please spare me. I can't face a lot of female blah-blah-blah right now. I know that kind of talk well, the enumeration of offenses, the balancing of idiotic totals. Right now I am more interested in knowing why that damn detective isn't here yet. Oh Lyuba, don't you realize that we are in deadly, deadly . . .

LYUBOV'

Stop the hysterics! I am ashamed of you. I always knew you were a coward. I'll never forget how you started crawling under this very rug when he began shooting.

TROSHCHEYKIN

This rug, Lyuba, had my blood on it. You forget: I fell, I was critically wounded. . . . Yes, my blood. Think back, just think back—we had to send it to the cleaner's afterwards.

LYUBOV'

You always were a coward. When my baby died, you were afraid of his poor little ghost, and took tranquilizers at night. When some fire chief gave you a vulgar bawling-out for your portrait of him, because you got some detail of his parade uniform wrong, you did it over without a word. When we were walking down Industrial Avenue one time, and a couple of guffawing hooligans were ambling along behind us, appraising my assets, you pretended you didn't hear anything, but your face was as white as . . . as a piece of veal.

TROSHCHEYKIN

Go on, go on. This is getting interesting! My God, how rude you are!

LYUBOV'

There've been a million cases like that, but perhaps your most elegant gesture in this vein was when you took advantage of your adversary's helpless condition to slap his cheek. By the way, I think you didn't even hit it but smacked poor Misha's hand instead.

TROSHCHEYKIN

I certainly did hit it—you can be quite sure of that. I hit it and how! But continue, please. I am most curious to see to what extremes you're capable of going. And today of all days . . . when a terrible event has happened and upset everything. . . . What an obnoxious bitch.

LYUBOV'

Thank God it happened, this event. It has given us a real jolt, and put a lot of things into focus. You are heartless, unfeeling, petty, morally vulgar, and an egoist the likes of which has never been seen before. . . . I guess I'm no great shakes either in my own way. But not because I am a "fishwife," as you chose to call me. If I am rude and short-tempered, it is because you have made me so. Oh, Alyosha, if only you weren't stuffed full of yourself to the exclusion of all air and light, you would probably be able to see what I've turned into during the past few years, and what a state I am in now.

TROSHCHEYKIN

Lyuba, I'm controlling myself, and you please do the same. I realize that a brutal night like this is upsetting and makes you say brutal things. But get a grip on yourself.

LYUBOV'

There's nothing to grip — it has all crumbled.

TROSHCHEYKIN

Nothing has crumbled. What are you dreaming up? Lyuba, snap out of it! The fact that now and then we . . . well, yell at each other doesn't mean we are unhappy. And right now we are like two cornered animals who bite at each other only because they feel cramped and frightened.

LYUBOV'

No, it's not true. It's not true. Our quarreling has nothing to do with it. I'll even tell you more: you have nothing to do with it. I'm perfectly willing to believe that you have been happy with me, because, even in the worst catastrophe, an egoist of your proportions will always find his ultimate refuge inside himself. I know perfectly well that if anything were to happen to me, you would of course be very distressed, but at the same time you'd give your feelings a quick shuffle to see if some little trump pops up for you, some advantage—be it ever so small—deriving from the fact of my death. And you'd find it, yes, you'd find it! Even if it's no more than the fact that life costs exactly half as much. Oh, of course I know that it would be quite subconscious and not so coarse—simply a little mental subsidy at a critical moment. . . . It's a horrid thing to say, but I am convinced that when our boy died, the thought did go through your head that now there would be one less worry. Nowhere will you find such crafty rascals as among impractical people. Naturally, though, I'm willing to concede that you love me in your own fashion.

TROSHCHEYKIN

This must all be a dream: this room, this dreadful night, this virago. I reject any other explanation.

LYUBOV'

And your art! Your art. . . . At first I really did think that you were a marvelous, dazzling, precious talent, but now I know your true worth.

TROSHCHEYKIN

What? I've never heard that one before.

LYUBOV'

You'll hear it now. You're a nothing, you're a spinning top, you're a sterile flower, you're an empty, slightly gilded nutshell, and you will never create anything but will always remain what you are, a provincial portrait-painter with dreams of some azure grotto.

TROSHCHEYKIN
Lyuba! Lyuba! This painting . . . do you think it's bad? Take a look. Is it bad?

LYUBOV'
It's not my opinion, it's everybody's opinion of you. And they are right, because pictures must be painted for others, not for the delectation of some voracious monster inside you.

TROSHCHEYKIN
Lyuba, you can't be serious. There's no other way—of course I must paint for my monster, my tapeworm, and for it alone.

LYUBOV'
For God's sake, don't start a debate. I'm tired and don't know what I'm saying, and you quibble over words.

TROSHCHEYKIN
Your criticism of my art, of what is most important and sacred to me, is so silly and unfair that all your other accusations become meaningless. You can abuse my life and my character all you want, and I'll agree with everything in advance, but this—this is outside your competence. So you'd better drop the subject.

LYUBOV'
You're right—it's useless for me to talk to you.

TROSHCHEYKIN
Absolutely useless. And, anyway, it's not the right moment. This night worries me far more than our entire past life. If

you're tired and can't think straight, then keep quiet, instead of . . . Lyuba, Lyuba, don't make me suffer any more than I'm suffering already.

LYUBOV'
What do you have to suffer about? Shame on you. Let's suppose the improbable happens, and Leonid Barbashin comes crashing through that door right now, or climbs in through that window, or emerges like a shadow from behind that screen. . . . Even if this were to happen, believe me, I have an extremely simple way of turning things around.

TROSHCHEYKIN
You do?

LYUBOV'
Oh, yes!

TROSHCHEYKIN
Namely?

LYUBOV'
You want to know?

TROSHCHEYKIN
Tell me, tell me.

LYUBOV'
Here's what I'll do: I'll shout that I love him, that it was all a mistake, that I'm ready to follow him to the ends of the earth. . . .

TROSHCHEYKIN
Yes. . . . But don't you think it's a bit . . . melodramatic? I

don't know. . . . What if he doesn't believe you, and realizes it's a trick? No, Lyuba, I just don't think it'll work. It may sound logical, but. . . . No, he'll feel insulted and kill us on the spot.

LYUBOV'
Is that all you have to tell me on the subject?

TROSHCHEYKIN
No, no—it's all wrong. No, Lyuba, it's somehow unartistic and flat. . . . I don't know. . . . Tell me, does that look to you like somebody standing over there on the other side? Further up, over there? Or is it only the shadow of leaves under the street lamp?

LYUBOV'
Is that all, Alyosha?

TROSHCHEYKIN
Yes, it's only a shadow.

LYUBOV'
You are exactly like the child in *Erlkönig*. And, what's more, this has happened before, all of it has happened just like this—you said "shadow," I said "child," and at that point Mother came in.

ANTONINA PAVLOVNA
I came to say goodnight. I want to go to bed early tonight.

LYUBOV'
Yes, I'm tired too.

ANTONINA PAVLOVNA
What a night. . . . What a wind!

TROSHCHEYKIN

Now, that's strange to say the least: it's so still out not even the proverbial leaf is stirring.

ANTONINA PAVLOVNA

Then it must be the ringing in my ears.

TROSHCHEYKIN

Or the whispering muse.

LYUBOV'

Alyosha, stop it.

TROSHCHEYKIN

Nice, pleasant situation, isn't it, Antonina Pavlovna? A scoundrel, who has sworn he will murder your daughter, is at large, perhaps at our very doorstep, while here we have a cozy family gathering, and swans perform high kicks, and the typewriter chatters merrily away. . . .

LYUBOV'

Alyosha, stop it this instant.

ANTONINA PAVLOVNA

My dear Alyosha, nothing you say can offend me, and, as for the danger, we are all in the hands of the Almighty.

TROSHCHEYKIN

I don't have much confidence in those hands.

ANTONINA PAVLOVNA

That, my friend, is why you're so pathetic and ill-tempered.

LYUBOV'
Come on, stop quarreling.

TROSHCHEYKIN
Oh well, Antonina Pavlovna, not everyone is blessed with Buddhist wisdom.
(The doorbell rings.)

TROSHCHEYKIN
Ah, thank heavens. That's my detective. Listen, Lyuba—I know it's silly of me, but I'm afraid to open the door.

LYUBOV'
All right, I'll open it.

TROSHCHEYKIN
No, no—wait a minute. . . . What's the best way to do it. . . .

ANTONINA PAVLOVNA
Why, has Marfa gone to bed already?

LYUBOV'
Marfa has left. Alyosha, let go of my hand.

ANTONINA PAVLOVNA
I'll open the door. You stay here. It would take more than a Barbashin to scare me.

TROSHCHEYKIN
Ask who it is through the door first.

LYUBOV'
I'll go with you, Mama.

(The bell rings again. Antonina Pavlovna goes off to the right.)

TROSHCHEYKIN
Strange . . . why does he ring so energetically? How unpleasant. . . . No, Lyuba, I will not let you go!

LYUBOV'
Yes, you will.

TROSHCHEYKIN
Stop it. Don't try to get away. I can't hear a thing.

LYUBOV'
You're hurting me.

TROSHCHEYKIN
Then stop twisting. Let me listen. What's going on? Can you hear?

LYUBOV'
What garbage you are, Alyosha!

TROSHCHEYKIN
Lyuba, we'd better go away. *(drags her to the left)*

LYUBOV'
What a coward. . . .

TROSHCHEYKIN
We can make it down the backstairs. . . . Don't you dare! Stop!
(She breaks away. Simultaneously Antonina Pavlovna comes in from the right.)

ANTONINA PAVLOVNA

You know, Lyubusha, there's still broken glass crunching underfoot in the hall.

TROSHCHEYKIN

Who was it?

ANTONINA PAVLOVNA

It's for you. Says you had him sent from a detective agency.

TROSHCHEYKIN

Ah—that's what I thought.
(Troshcheykin goes out.)

ANTONINA PAVLOVNA

Quite a strange character. First thing he did was go to the bathroom.

LYUBOV'

You shouldn't have let him in.

ANTONINA PAVLOVNA

What could I do—after all, Alyosha did place an order for him. I must tell you, Lyuba, I am sincerely sorry for your husband.

LYUBOV'

Oh, Mama—let's stop snapping at each other all the time.

ANTONINA PAVLOVNA

You look terribly tired. . . . Go to bed, my sweet.

LYUBOV'

Yes, I'll go soon. Alyosha and I will probably still have to

finish our fight. What does he think he's doing—inviting a detective into the house.
(Troshcheykin returns.)

TROSHCHEYKIN
Antonina Pavlovna, where is he? What did you do with him? Can't find him anywhere.

ANTONINA PAVLOVNA
I told you—he went to wash his hands.

TROSHCHEYKIN
You didn't tell me anything. *(goes out)*

ANTONINA PAVLOVNA
You know, Lyubinka—I think I'll be off to bed. Good night. I want to thank you, darling. . . .

LYUBOV'
For what?

ANTONINA PAVLOVNA
Well, for the birthday celebration. I thought it was all a great success, didn't you?

LYUBOV'
Of course it was a success.

ANTONINA PAVLOVNA
There were lots of people. Lots of excitement. Even that Shnap woman wasn't too bad.

LYUBOV'
Well, I'm very glad you had a good time. . . . Mummy!

ANTONINA PAVLOVNA
Yes?

LYUBOV'
Mummy, I just had a horrible thought! Are you sure it was a detective who came and not . . . someone else?

ANTONINA PAVLOVNA
Rubbish. He immediately stuck his photograph in my hand. I think I gave it to Alyosha. No—here it is.

LYUBOV'
What kind of nonsense is this? . . . Why does he hand around his picture?

ANTONINA PAVLOVNA
I don't know—probably they're supposed to—

LYUBOV'
Why is he in a medieval costume? What is this—King Lear? "To my respecters: my respects." What kind of tomfoolery *is* this?

ANTONINA PAVLOVNA
He said he was from the detective agency. That's all I know. It must be some kind of secret sign. . . . Tell me, did you hear what our writer said about my story?

LYUBOV'
No.

ANTONINA PAVLOVNA
That it is something halfway between a poem in prose and prose in verse. I think it was a compliment. What do you say?

LYUBOV'
Of course it was a compliment.

ANTONINA PAVLOVNA
And did you like it?

LYUBOV'
Very much.

ANTONINA PAVLOVNA
Only some parts or the whole thing?

LYUBOV'
The whole thing, the whole thing. Mummy, in a moment I'm going to burst into tears. Please go to bed.

ANTONINA PAVLOVNA
Would you like some of my drops?

LYUBOV'
I don't want anything. I want to die.

ANTONINA PAVLOVNA
You know what your mood reminds me of?

LYUBOV'
Please, Mummy. . . .

ANTONINA PAVLOVNA
No, it's a strange thing. . . . You were nineteen, and crazy about Barbashin, and would come home more dead than alive, and I was afraid to say a word to you.

LYUBOV'

In that case you ought to be afraid now, too.

ANTONINA PAVLOVNA

Promise me you won't do anything rash or unreasonable. Promise me, Lyubinka!

LYUBOV'

Is it any of your business? Stop nagging me.

ANTONINA PAVLOVNA

I am not afraid of the same thing as Alyosha. I fear something very different.

LYUBOV'

And I'm telling you: leave me alone! You live in your world, and I live in mine. Let's not try to set up interplanetary communications. Nothing will come of it anyway.

ANTONINA PAVLOVNA

I am very sad that you withdraw into yourself like this. I often think you are unfair toward Alyosha. You have to admit he is a very good man and worships you.

LYUBOV'

What is this, a tactical maneuver?

ANTONINA PAVLOVNA

No, it's just that I keep remembering certain things. . . . Your insanity at the time, and what Father used to say to you.

LYUBOV'

Good night.

ANTONINA PAVLOVNA

And now somehow it's happening all over again. May the good Lord help you overcome it this time, too.

LYUBOV'

Stop it, stop it, stop it. . . . It's you yourself who are involving me in some turbid, viscous, trite staging of the senses. I don't want it. What does it have to do with you? Alyosha plagues me with his fears, and you with yours. Leave me alone, both of you. Keep away from me. Who cares if for six years I've been squeezed and stretched until I turned into some kind of gazelle-like provincial vamp, huge eyes and nothing else? I don't want it. And, furthermore, what right do *you* have to interrogate me? After all, you really couldn't care less—you just gather momentum and then can't stop. . . .

ANTONINA PAVLOVNA

Just one question, then I'll go to bed: are you going to see him?

LYUBOV'

I shall send the nurse with a note in French.[7] I'll fly to him. I'll leave my husband. I'll . . .

ANTONINA PAVLOVNA

Lyuba, you're . . . you're joking, aren't you?

LYUBOV'

Yes. It's a draft for the third act.

ANTONINA PAVLOVNA

I hope to God he has fallen out of love with you during these years—if not, we're in for no end of trouble.

---

[7] An allusion to *Eugene Onegin.*

LYUBOV'

Mother, stop it! Stop, do you hear?
(Troshcheykin enters from the right and turns back to speak in the direction of the door.)

TROSHCHEYKIN

In here, please. . . .

ANTONINA PAVLOVNA
(to Lyubov')
Good night. God bless you.

TROSHCHEYKIN

Why did you get stuck out there in the hallway? These are just old magazines, just rubbish—don't bother with them.

ANTONINA PAVLOVNA

Good night, Alyosha.

TROSHCHEYKIN

Sleep well, sleep well. *(toward the door)* In here, please.
(Antonina Pavlovna goes out. Enter Barboshin. He is wearing sporty clothes: a checked suit consisting of jacket and plus fours; but he has a tragic actor's head, with long grayish-red hair. His movements are slow and sweeping. He is solemnly absentminded. He is a detective with a Dostoyevskian flawed soul. He enters, and bows deeply to Lyubov'.)

BARBOSHIN

I bow not to you, no, not to you, but to all wives who are deceived, strangled, and burned, and to the lovely adulteresses of the last century beneath their veils thick as night itself.

TROSHCHEYKIN

This is my studio. The attempted murder took place in here. I fear that he will be attracted precisely to this room.

BARBOSHIN

You child! What enchanting, philistine naiveté! No, the place of the crime attracted criminals only until that fact became the property of the general public. When a wild canyon becomes a resort, the eagles fly away. *(with another deep bow to Lyubov')* I bow also to reticent wives, to pensive ones. . . . I bow to the enigma of womanhood. . . .

LYUBOV'

Alyosha, what does this gentleman want from me?

TROSHCHEYKIN
(softly)
Don't be afraid, everything is under control. This is the best man the local private detective agency could give me.

BARBOSHIN

Those who are in love should be advised that I have been trained to hear asides even more clearly than normal speech. This shoe has been bothering me for a long time. *(pulls it off)*

TROSHCHEYKIN

I also wanted you to investigate the window.

BARBOSHIN
(investigating the shoe)
Just as I thought: a nail. Yes, you gave your spouse a correct description of me. This past spring I had a particularly successful season. A small hammer, or something. . . . All right, give me that. . . . Incidentally, I had one most

interesting assignment right here on your street. A case of ultra-adultery, type B, Series 18. Unfortunately, for obvious reasons of professional ethics, I cannot name any names. But I'm sure you know her: Mrs. Tamára Grékov, age 23, blond, with pomeranian dog.

TROSHCHEYKIN
The window, please. . . .

BARBOSHIN

Excuse me for limiting myself to hints. The secret of the confessional. But back to business. What is it you don't like about this excellent window?

TROSHCHEYKIN
Look: right next to it is a drainpipe along which it's very easy to climb up.

BARBOSHIN
The counter-client could break his neck.

TROSHCHEYKIN
He's agile as a monkey!

BARBOSHIN

In that case, I can suggest a certain secret method, employed infrequently but to good effect. You will be pleased. The thing to do is install a so-called False Cornice, i.e., a cornice or window ledge that detaches at the slightest pressure. It comes with a three-year guarantee. Is the implication clear?

TROSHCHEYKIN
Yes, but how shall we go about it? . . . Workmen will be needed. . . . It's late!

BARBOSHIN

Oh, it's not so important; anyway, I'll be walking under your windows until dawn, as we agreed. Incidentally, you'll find it quite curious to watch how I do it. Instructive and fascinating. In short, only dunces walk to and fro like a pendulum. I do it this way. *(walks)* I walk in a preoccupied manner along one side of the street, then cross to the other on a reverse diagonal. . . . So. . . . And, just as preoccupied, walk along the other side. Thus, initially, you get the letter "N." Then I traverse on the opposite diagonal, making a cross . . . so . . . returning to the point of departure, and then I repeat the whole process. Now: you see that I always move along both sidewalks in the same direction, thereby achieving inconspicuousness and naturalness. This is Dr. Rubini's method. There are others.

LYUBOV'

Alyosha, send him home. He gives me the creeps. I'm going to scream in a minute.

BARBOSHIN

There is absolutely no need to worry, Madam. You may go beddy-bye without a worry in the world, and, in case of insomnia, observe my movements from your window. There's a full moon tonight, and it'll be very effective. One further observation: I generally receive an advance, as the party under protection sometimes suddenly disappears for no reason at all. . . . But you are so beautiful, the night so moonlit, that I feel somehow embarrassed to broach the subject.

TROSHCHEYKIN

Well, thank you. This is all very comforting.

BARBOSHIN

What else. . . . Hey, listen, what about those paintings—are you sure they are not fakes?

TROSHCHEYKIN

No, they are mine. Painted them myself.

BARBOSHIN

So they *are* fakes! You know, you really ought to consult an expert. Now tell me—what would you like me to undertake tomorrow?

TROSHCHEYKIN

Tomorrow morning, about eight, you'll come up and see me. By the way, here's the key. Then we'll decide what to do next.

BARBOSHIN

I have grandiose plans! Did you know that I am able to eavesdrop on the counter-client's thoughts? Yes, tomorrow I'll be shadowing his intentions. What is his last name? I think you told me. . . . It began with "Sh." Do you happen to remember?

TROSHCHEYKIN

Leonid Viktorovich Barbashin.

BARBOSHIN

No, no—don't mix things up: the name is Barboshin, Al'fred Afanasyevich.

LYUBOV'

Can't you see, Alyosha? He's a sick man.

TROSHCHEYKIN

The man who threatens us is named Barbashin.

BARBOSHIN

And I'm telling you my name is Barboshin. Al'fred
Barboshin. Which is, incidentally, one of my many authentic
names. Mmm—what marvelous plans! Oh, you'll see! Life
will be beautiful. Life will taste good. Birds will sing among
the sticky young leaves, the blind shall hear, and the
deaf-and-dumb shall see. Young women shall lift up their
raspberry-colored infants to the sun. Yesterday's enemies
shall embrace each other. And the enemies of their enemies.
And the enemies of their children. And the children of their
enemies. You only have to believe. . . . Now give me a
straight and simple answer: do you have a gun in the house?

TROSHCHEYKIN

No, alas! I would have gotten one, but I don't know how to
use it. I'm afraid even to touch a gun. You must understand
that I am an artist. I don't know how to do anything.

BARBOSHIN

I recognize my youth in you. I was like that too—a poet, a
student, a dreamer. . . . Under the chestnut trees of
Heidelberg I loved an amazon. . . . But life has taught me
many things. O.K. Let's not stir up the past. *(sings)* "Well,
shall we start. . . ."[8] All right—I'm off to walk beneath your
windows, while over you hover Cupid, Morpheus, and little
Valium. Tell me, Mister—you don't happen to have a
cigarette, do you?

[8]Sung by Onegin before the duel in the opera *Eugene Onegin.*
Tchaikovsky's tune should, of course, be used.

TROSHCHEYKIN

I'm a nonsmoker myself . . . but I saw some somewhere. . . .
Lyuba, Ryovshin forgot a pack here this morning. Where is
it? Oh, here.

BARBOSHIN

It will cheer me up during my hours of vigil. Only take me
out the back way, through the yard. It's more proper that way.

TROSHCHEYKIN

Oh, in that case, this way please.

BARBOSHIN

(bowing deeply to Lyubov')
I bow, also, to all the misunderstood . . .

LYUBOV'

All right, I'll pass it on.

BARBOSHIN

I thank you.
*(leaves with Troshcheykin to the left. Lyubov' is alone for a few
seconds. Troshcheykin returns hurriedly.)*

TROSHCHEYKIN

Matches! Where are the matches? He needs matches.

LYUBOV'

For God's sake, get him out of here quick. Where is he?

TROSHCHEYKIN

I left him on the back stairs. I'll see him out and be back in a
minute. Don't worry. The matches!

LYUBOV'

There they are, right under your nose.

TROSHCHEYKIN

I don't know about you, Lyuba, but my spirits are a lot better after that conversation. He seems to be a great expert in his field, and there's something very original and cozy about him. Don't you think so?

LYUBOV'

As far as I'm concerned, he's insane. Go.

TROSHCHEYKIN

Be right back.
(Troshcheykin runs off to the left. Lyubov' is alone for about three seconds. The doorbell rings. At first she freezes, then quickly goes off to the right. The stage remains empty. Through the open door can be heard the voice of Meshaev Two, and presently he enters, carrying a basket of apples, and accompanied by Lyubov'. His appearance can be deduced from the following dialogue.)

MESHAEV TWO

So you're sure I didn't make a mistake? Mrs. Opayashin does live here?

LYUBOV'

Yes, she's my mother.

MESHAEV TWO

Ah! Glad to know you.

LYUBOV'

You can put it here. . . .

MESHAEV TWO

Oh, don't bother—I'll just place it on the floor. . . . You see, my brother told me to come here as soon as I arrived. Is he here yet? Don't tell me I'm the first guest?

LYUBOV'

Actually, we expected you in the afternoon, for tea. But that's all right. Let me go look—I'm sure Mama isn't asleep yet.

MESHAEV TWO

Oh my Lord—did I get it all wrong? What a snafu! Forgive me. . . . I'm awfully embarrassed. Don't wake her, please. Here, I've brought some apples—please give them to her, and ask her to excuse me. I'll be running along. . . .

LYUBOV'

No, no—I won't hear of it. Do sit down. If only she's not asleep, she'll be very glad.
(Troshcheykin enters and stops in his tracks.)

LYUBOV'

Alyosha, this is Osip Mikheyevich's brother.

TROSHCHEYKIN

Brother? Oh, yes, of course. Welcome.

MESHAEV TWO

I feel so guilty. . . . I don't have the honor of knowing Mrs. Opayashin personally. But a few days ago I informed Osip that I would be coming here on business, and yesterday he answers to shoot right over from the station to the birthday party—we'll meet there, he says.

LYUBOV'
I'll go tell her right away. *(goes out)*

MESHAEV TWO
Since I'd written him that I was coming on the evening express train, I naturally concluded from his answer that Mrs. Opayashin's party was in the evening, too. Either I wrote him the wrong arrival time or he didn't pay attention to my letter, which is more likely. Hell of a shame. So you must be her son?

TROSHCHEYKIN
Son-in-law.

MESHAEV TWO
Ah, the husband of this charming lady. So. I see you're amazed by my resemblance to my brother.

TROSHCHEYKIN
Oh, well, you know—nothing could amaze me today. I'm in bad trouble. . . .

MESHAEV TWO
Yes, everybody's complaining. If only you lived in the country!

TROSHCHEYKIN
Actually, the resemblance *is* amazing.

MESHAEV TWO
Today, quite by chance, I ran into a joker I hadn't seen since I was a boy. He once made a comment to the effect that both I and my brother were played by one and the same actor, only in the part of my brother he was good, and in mine he was bad.

TROSHCHEYKIN

You seem to be balder.

MESHAEV TWO

Alas! Bald as a billiard ball, as they say.

TROSHCHEYKIN

Excuse me for yawning. It's a purely nervous phenomenon.

MESHAEV TWO

City life—there's nothing you can do. As for me, I haven't budged from my blessed wilderness for close on to ten years now. Don't read the papers, raise shaggy-legged chickens, have oodles of kiddies, an orchard, a wife that big. Came to town to shop for a tractor. Are you and my brother close friends? Or did you only meet him at your mother-in-law's?

TROSHCHEYKIN

Yes, at my mother—ex-ca-a-use me, pa-pa-please. . . . *(yawns)*

MESHAEV TWO

Don't mention it. Yes. . . . He and I don't hit it off too well together. Haven't seen him in a good long while—several years—and, to be frank, the separation has never been much of a burden to either of us. But since I *was* coming, it would have been awkward not to let him know. I'm beginning to think he deliberately behaved like a pig toward me: and that's as far as his knowledge of pig-raising goes.

TROSHCHEYKIN

Yes, that's not unusual. . . . I don't know much about it either. . . .

MESHAEV TWO

I gather from his letter that Mrs. Opayashin is a literary

figure? Alas, I don't keep up much with literature.

TROSHCHEYKIN
Oh, well, you know, her kind of literature is unremarkable.
Oh-ha-a-a. *(yawns)*

MESHAEV TWO
And apparently does some drawing, too.

TROSHCHEYKIN
No, no—this is *my* studio.

MESHAEV TWO
Oh, so you're a picture-painter! That's interesting. I've
done a bit of that myself in the winter, to pass the time.
Also used to fool around with the occult sciences at one time.
So these are your paintings. . . . May I have a look? *(puts on
a pince-nez)*

TROSHCHEYKIN
Go ahead. *(pause)* This one isn't finished.

MESHAEV TWO
Very good! A daring brush.

TROSHCHEYKIN
Excuse me, I'd like to take a look out the window.

MESHAEV TWO
(returning the pince-nez to its case)
It's such a shame. How embarrassing—to have your
mother-in-law dragged out of bed because of me. After all,
she doesn't even know me. I sailed in under my brother's
flag.

TROSHCHEYKIN

Look, how amusing.

MESHAEV TWO

I don't understand. The moon, the street. I'd sooner say it was melancholy.

TROSHCHEYKIN

Look—he's walking. There! He's crossed. And again. Most comforting sight.

MESHAEV TWO

A belated reveler. I hear they do a lot of drinking in this town.
(Enter Antonina Pavlovna and Lyubov' carrying a tray.)

ANTONINA PAVLOVNA

Goodness, what a likeness!

MESHAEV TWO

Honored. . . . Happy birthday. . . . I took the liberty. . . . They're from my farm.

ANTONINA PAVLOVNA

Shame on you for spoiling me like this. Sit down, please. My daughter has explained everything.

MESHAEV TWO

I'm very embarrassed. Surely you were resting?

ANTONINA PAVLOVNA

Oh, I'm a night owl. Come, tell me about yourself. So you spend all your time in the country?

TROSHCHEYKIN

Lyuba, isn't that the phone?

LYUBOV'

Yes, I think so. I'll go. . . .

TROSHCHEYKIN

No, I'll go.

(Troshcheykin goes out.)

MESHAEV TWO

Never budge. Raise chickens, produce children, don't read the papers.

ANTONINA PAVLOVNA

Cup of tea? Or would you rather have a snack?

MESHAEV TWO

Well, actually . . .

ANTONINA PAVLOVNA

Lyuba, there's some ham left. Oh, you brought it already. Fine. Help yourself. It's Mikhey Mikheyevich, right?

MESHAEV TWO

Much obliged. Yes, Mikhey's the name.

ANTONINA PAVLOVNA

Please help yourself. We had cake but the guests ate it all. We were looking forward so much to your coming! Your brother thought you had missed your train. Lyuba, there isn't enough sugar here. *(to Mikhey Mikheyevich)* Today, due to the event, our household is a little out of kilter.

MESHAEV TWO
The event?

ANTONINA PAVLOVNA
Oh, you know—today's sensation. We're so worried. . . .

LYUBOV'
Mummy, dear, Mr. Meshaev couldn't care less about our private business.

ANTONINA PAVLOVNA
I thought he knew. In any case, I'm delighted that you arrived. On a nervous night like this it's good to have some one calm around.

MESHAEV TWO
Yup. You might say I've grown unaccustomed to your city alarms.

ANTONINA PAVLOVNA
Where are you staying?

MESHAEV TWO
Well . . . nowhere, for the time being. I guess I'll go to a hotel.

ANTONINA PAVLOVNA
Why don't you spend the night with us? We have a spare room—this one.

MESHAEV TWO
I really don't know. . . . I wouldn't want to impose. . . .
(Troshcheykin returns.)

TROSHCHEYKIN

Ryovshin called. It seems he and Kuprikov have posted themselves at a little bar nearby, and wanted to know if all was well. I think they're loaded. I told them they could go to bed, since we have this *simpatico* fellow marching up and down in front of our house. *(to Meshaev Two)* See what things have come to? We had to hire a guardian angel.

MESHAEV TWO

That so?

LYUBOV'

Alyosha, find some other subject, will you?

TROSHCHEYKIN

What are you angry about? I think it was very nice of them to call. Unlike your dear sister, who didn't even bother to find out if we were alive.

MESHAEV TWO

I'm afraid you must have family troubles of some kind. . . . Someone must be ill. . . . I'm doubly distressed.

TROSHCHEYKIN

No, no—please stay. On the contrary, it's better to have a crowd hanging around. Anyway, sleep is out of the question.

MESHAEV TWO

That so?

ANTONINA PAVLOVNA

The fact of the matter is that—rightly or not—Alexey Maximovich fears an attempt on his life. He has enemies. . . . After all, Lyubochka, you have to give a person some explanation . . . or else, seeing you rush around like two lunatics . . . God knows what he'll think.

MESHAEV TWO

Oh, don't you worry about it. I understand. I was just being tactful. They say that in Paris, France, they also have this Bohemian life, fights in restaurants, and so forth. . . .
(Barboshin has entered noiselessly and unnoticed. They all give a start.)

TROSHCHEYKIN

Why do you scare the wits out of us like that? What happened?

BARBOSHIN

I came in to take a breather.

ANTONINA PAVLOVNA
(to Meshaev Two)
Please don't get up. It's nothing. A secret agent.

TROSHCHEYKIN

Did you notice anything? Maybe you'd like to talk to me privately?

BARBOSHIN

No, Mister. I crave a little light, a little warmth. . . . I was beginning to get the willies. It's lonely and scary out there. Nerves are starting to give. . . . Torments of the imagination, an uneasy conscience, images from the past. . . .

LYUBOV'

Alyosha, it's either him or me. You give him a glass of tea — I'm going to bed.

BARBOSHIN

(to Meshaev Two)

Aha! And who is this? How did you get in here?

MESHAEV TWO

Me? Why, I came in the usual way — through the door.

BARBOSHIN

(to Troshcheykin)

Mister, I consider this a personal insult. Either I guard you and screen all visitors, or I go home and you receive your guests. . . . Or maybe he is from a rival organization?

TROSHCHEYKIN

Take it easy. It's just somebody from out of town. He didn't know. Here, take an apple and go, please. One doesn't abandon one's post. You were doing so beautifully until now! . . .

BARBOSHIN

I was promised a glass of tea. I'm tired. I'm chilled. There's a nail in my shoe. *(narrating)* I was born into a poor family, and my first conscious recollection is —

LYUBOV'

You'll get your tea, but under one condition — that you shut up, shut up completely!

BARBOSHIN

Since you ask me . . . what can I do but comply? I only wanted to give you a capsule history of my life. As an illustration. No?

ANTONINA PAVLOVNA

Lyuba, how can you cut off a person like that?

LYUBOV'
No life histories, or I'm leaving.

BARBOSHIN
May I at least deliver a telegram?

TROSHCHEYKIN
A telegram? Where from? Quick, let's have it!

BARBOSHIN
I just intercepted its bearer right near the downstairs entrance. Lordy, Lordy—what did I do with it? Ah! Here it is.

TROSHCHEYKIN
(grabs the telegram and opens it)
"My thoughts are with you birthday gree—" What rubbish! You could have spared yourself the trouble. *(to Antonina Pavlovna)* It's for you.

ANTONINA PAVLOVNA
You see, Lyubochka—you were right. Misha did remember!

MESHAEV TWO
It's getting late! Time to hit the sack. I apologize once again.

ANTONINA PAVLOVNA
Won't you spend the night with us after all?

TROSHCHEYKIN
Hear, hear! You can sleep right there on the couch.

MESHAEV TWO
Actually, I . . .

BARBOSHIN
(to Meshaev Two)
Judging by certain outward signs intelligible only to an experienced eye, I can tell you that you have served in the navy, are childless, have recently been to the doctor, and are fond of music.

MESHAEV TWO
Wrong on all counts.

BARBOSHIN
Moreover, you are left-handed.

MESHAEV TWO
Wrong again.

BARBOSHIN
Tell it to the judge. He'll know right away.

LYUBOV'
(to Meshaev Two)
Please don't think this is a loony bin we have here. It's just been that kind of day and now it's that kind of night.

MESHAEV TWO
Oh, I don't mind.

ANTONINA PAVLOVNA
(to Barboshin)
There are many things about your profession that appeal to a writer of fiction. I'd be very curious to know your attitude toward the detective novel as such.

BARBOSHIN
There are questions I am under no obligation to answer.

MESHAEV TWO
(to Lyubov')
You know, it's odd: this gentleman's attempt at divination together with a remarkable encounter I just had brings to mind how once, for lack of anything better to do, I took up fortune-telling—on an amateur level, of course, but sometimes with considerable success.

LYUBOV'
Do you do palm-reading?

TROSHCHEYKIN
Oh, if you could only predict what will become of us! Here we are sitting joking—a feast during the plague—and all the time I have a feeling that any minute we may be blown sky-high. *(to Barboshin)* For Christ's sake, finish your stupid tea!

BARBOSHIN
It's not stupid at all.

ANTONINA PAVLOVNA
Not long ago I read a book by a certain Hindu author. He gives amazing examples. . . .

TROSHCHEYKIN
Unfortunately I can't live very long in a state of amazement. I think my hair is going to turn gray overnight.

MESHAEV TWO
That so?

LYUBOV'
Would you tell my fortune?

MESHAEV TWO

Glad to. Only I haven't done this for a long time. Cold little hand you have.

TROSHCHEYKIN

Predict a journey for her, I implore you.

MESHAEV TWO

What curious lines. The life line, for example. . . . Actually, you ought to have died a long time ago. How old are you? Twenty-two, twenty-three?

(Barboshin starts slowly and somewhat diffidently to examine his own palm.)

LYUBOV'

Twenty-five. I survived by a fluke.

MESHAEV TWO

Your reason is obedient to your heart, but your heart is a rational one. Well, what else can I tell you? You have a feeling for nature, but are rather indifferent to art.

TROSHCHEYKIN

True enough.

MESHAEV TWO

You will die. . . . You're not afraid to learn how you will die?

LYUBOV'

Not a bit. Tell me.

MESHAEV TWO

There's a certain bifurcation here, though, that perplexes me. . . . No, I won't venture to give an exact answer.

BARBOSHIN
(proffering his palm)
Here's mine.

LYUBOV'
Well, you certainly didn't tell me very much. I thought you would predict something extraordinary, something startling . . . for instance, that my life has reached an abyss, that an incredible, fearful, magical happiness awaits me. . . .

TROSHCHEYKIN
Quiet! I thought I heard somebody ring. . . . Eh?

BARBOSHIN
(thrusting his hand toward Meshaev Two)
Here's mine.

ANTONINA PAVLOVNA
No, you're hearing things. Poor Alyosha, poor dear. . . . Take it easy, darling.

MESHAEV TWO
(mechanically taking Barboshin's palm)
You ask too much of me, dear lady. The hand is sometimes reticent. Of course, there are garrulous, outspoken palms. Ten years ago I predicted all kinds of disasters for a man, and today, just a short while ago, as I was getting off the train, I suddenly see him on the station platform. Turned out he had spent several years in jail, because of some romantic brawl, and was now going abroad for good. A certain Barbashin, Leonid Barbashin. It was strange, running into him and then saying good-by right away. *(leans over the hand of Barboshin, who is also sitting with lowered head)*

He asked me to say hello to our mutual friends, but you wouldn't know him, I'm sure. . . .

CURTAIN

The Pole

DRAMA IN ONE ACT

INTRODUCTORY NOTE

The first version of *The Pole (Polyus)* was completed at the Domaine de Beaulieu, Solliès-Pont, Var (near Toulon), on 8 July 1923. It was revised in Berlin in April of 1924. The present text is a collation of two handwritten transcriptions, representing slightly different versions, from the albums of Vladimir Nabokov's mother, and of the play as published in two installments in *Rul'* in Berlin, 14 and 16 August 1924, with a few minor supplementary corrections of what were obvious oversights or misprints.

CAST OF CHARACTERS

Captain Scott
Fleming
Kingsley
Johnson

"He was a very gallant gentleman" (from Scott's notebook)

*Interior of a tent. Four figures: Captain Scott, dubbed "Chief,"
and Fleming semi-reclining; Kingsley and Johnson asleep, totally
bundled up. All four have their legs in fur bags.*

FLEMING
Only twelve miles to go—yet we must wait. . . .
What a snowstorm . . . it roves, it tears. . . . Still writing,
Chief?

CAPT. SCOTT
(leafing through his diary)
      Yes, it must be done. . . . It's forty-four
days now since we departed from the pole,
and it is the fifth day that we have been
held captive by the storm inside this tent,
and have no food. . . .

JOHNSON
(sleepily)
          Oh. . . .

CAPT. SCOTT
You're awake? How are
you feeling?

JOHNSON
Not too bad. . . . It's curious. . . .
It seems as if I'm split into two parts —
one is myself, strong, lucid . . . while the other's
scorbutic, drowsy . . . a real sleepyhead. . . .

CAPT. SCOTT
How about a little water?

JOHNSON
No, no thanks. . . .
Another thing: I had a dream when I
was little — I still remember — that my feet,
when I looked down, had turned into the feet of
an elephant. *(laughs)*
I guess my dream's come true now.
How's Kingsley?

CAPT. SCOTT
Bad, I gather — he was raving. . .
but now he's still.

JOHNSON
When we are all back home
we'll organize a banquet . . . what a banquet —
we'll have a turkey and, above all, speeches,
speeches. . . .

CAPT. SCOTT

       I know — you could pass for a turkey
yourself, when you get really good and drunk!
Eh, Johnson?
         He's already asleep. . . .

FLEMING

               Just think —
twelve miles between us and the coast, the inlet,
where, tilting to one side its hoary masts,
amid blue icebergs waits our ship! I can
see it so clearly! . . .

CAPT. SCOTT

        Well, what can we do,
Fleming? Our luck ran out. That's all. . . .

FLEMING

                And only
twelve miles to go! Chief, I don't know — what do
you think: after the blizzard has abated,
could we, dragging the sick on sleds behind
us, make it back? . . .

CAPT. SCOTT

       I doubt it. . . .

FLEMING

             Right. And if . . .
If they weren't there?

CAPT. SCOTT

       Forget that. . . . Who knows all

the things one can conceive of. . . . Would you check
the time, my friend.

FLEMING

You're right, Chief. . . . It is six
past one. . . .

CAPT. SCOTT

Oh, well—we can hold out until
nightfall. . . . You realize, Fleming—after all,
they're looking for us, coming from the coast
to meet us. . . . Maybe stumble on us. . . .
Meanwhile let's sleep. . . . It will be easier. . . .

FLEMING

I don't feel sleepy.

CAPT. SCOTT

In that case, you'll wake me—
say—in an hour. Or else I might just lapse,
just lapse. . . . Oh well, you understand. . . .

FLEMING

Aye, aye, Chief.

(pause)

All three asleep. . . . Lucky for them. . . . To whom, then,
can I explain that I am strong and avid,
that I could gobble up not twelve but hundreds
of miles, so stubborn is the life within me.
My hunger and the icy wind have forced
all of my strength into one burning, bursting
mote. . . . And there is nothing in the world
a mote like that cannot achieve. . . .

(pause)

Johnson,
what is it? Do you need some help?

JOHNSON

I'll manage, don't
worry. . . . I'm going outside, Fleming. . . .

FLEMING

Where?

JOHNSON

Oh, I just want to have a look if there
is anything in sight. I may well be
some time. . . .

FLEMING

Take care — don't lose your bearings in
the blizzard. . . .

Gone. . . . A miracle that he's
still capable of walking, with his feet
already rotting. . . .
(pause)

What a storm! The whole
tent shudders from the snowy din. . . .

KINGSLEY
(delirious)

Oh, Jessie,
my darling — It's so beautiful. . . . We've seen
the pole, and I have brought you back a penguin.
Here, Jessie — you just take a look how smoo-
smoo-smooth he is . . . and how he waddles. . . . Jessie,
you're honeysuckle. . . . *(laughs)*

FLEMING
                                 Lucky man. . . . I have
no one to be delirious about. . . .
The Captain has a wife and little son
in London. Kingsley has a fiancée,
almost a widow. . . . Johnson, I don't know —
I think his mother. . . . What a notion to
go walking. Funny chap, that Johnson, really.
To him life is a mixture of exploit
and prank. . . . He knows no doubts, his soul is straight as
the shadow of a post on level snow. . . .
A lucky man. . . . While I must be a coward. . . .
Danger enticed me, but aren't women enticed
like that by an abyss? My life's not been
much good. . . . I've been a ship's boy and a diver,
hurled my harpoon upon uncharted seas. Oh,
those years of seafaring, of wandering,
of longing. . . . Few have been the peaceful nights,
the happy days I've had from life . . . and yet. . . .

KINGSLEY
(delirious)
Come on, come on! That's it, nice going! Hurry!
Don't dawdle, shoot — shoot at the goal! . . . Our Father,
Which art . . . *(mumbles)*

FLEMING
                           And yet I've an unbearable
desire to live. . . . Yes, to pursue a ball,
a woman, or the sun or — still more simply —
to eat, to eat a lot, to tear the plump
sardines in golden oil out of their tin. . . .
I want to live so much, it maddens me,
it hurts — to live somehow. . . .

CAPT. SCOTT

What's that? Who's there?
What happened?

FLEMING

Nothing, Chief. Everything's quiet. . . .
Except for Kingsley—he's delirious. . . .

CAPT. SCOTT
I had a kind of radiant, fearful dream. . . .
Where's Johnson?

FLEMING

Gone, to have a look if there
are rescuers in sight.

CAPT. SCOTT

How long ago?

FLEMING
By now, I'd say it's twenty minutes.

CAPT. SCOTT

Fleming,
you really shouldn't have let him go outside. . . .
However. . . . Hurry, hurry, help me up—
we're going out.

FLEMING

I'm sorry, Chief—I thought . . .

CAPT. SCOTT
No, it is not your fault.

Look at that snow!
(They go out together.)
(pause)

KINGSLEY
(alone, delirious)
Don't push — I can do it myself. . . . Stop it,
I don't need to be pushed. . . . *(raises himself up)*
Chief, Fleming, Johnson!
Hey, Chief! . . . No one. . . . Ah yes, I understand —
all three of them are gone. They must have thought
that I was dead already. . . . They have left me,
they have set out. . . .
No! It must be a joke!
Wait, please come back. . . . I have something to tell you. . . .
I want to tell. . . . So — this is what death means: a
glass entrance . . . water . . . water . . . it's all clear.
(pause)
(Capt. Scott and Fleming return.)

CAPT. SCOTT
How silly — I can't use my feet.
Oh, thanks. . . .
No matter. Not much chance of finding Johnson
in any case. . . . You realize what he's done?

FLEMING
Of course. . . . He weakened, fell — called, helplessly,
perhaps. . . . All this is very frightening. . . . *(goes back
into the depths of the tent)*

CAPT. SCOTT
(aside)

That's wrong—he did not call. He only thought
that, being sick, he was a burden to
the rest, and so he left. . . . It was so simple,
so valorous. . . . My bag is like a rock—
I can't get into it. . . .

FLEMING

                  Chief, this is dreadful—
Kingsley is dead. . . . Look at him. . . .

CAPT. SCOTT

                        My poor Eric!
Why did I have to bring him with me? He was
the youngest one of us. . . . Remember how
he cried when he discovered, at the pole, the
Norwegian flag? . . . The body can stay here—
don't touch it. . . .
(pause)

FLEMING

             We are left alone now, Chief. . . .

CAPT. SCOTT

But not for long, my friend, but not for long. . . .

FLEMING

The blizzard's dying down. . . .

CAPT. SCOTT

                 You know, I was just
thinking—Columbus, for example. . . . True,
he suffered, but, in recompense, discovered
such splendid lands, while we have suffered to

discover only ruinous white deserts —
and still, you know, it had to be. . . .

FLEMING

Well, Chief,
what if we tried to make a go for it?
Only twelve miles, and we'll be saved. . . .

CAPT. SCOTT

No, Fleming —
I can't get up. . . .

FLEMING

We have a sled. . . .

CAPT. SCOTT

You'd never
make it with me — I'm heavy. I am better
off here. It's peaceful. And so is my soul —
like Sunday in a Scottish townlet . . . feet
just hurt a little — and often they're a wee
bit tedious, our slow Sundays. . . . Pity we
don't have a chess set — we could have. . . .

FLEMING

Yes, pity. . . .

CAPT. SCOTT
Now listen, Fleming — you go by yourself. . . .

FLEMING
And leave you here alone? Weak as you are. . . .
You said yourself you might not last the night. . . .

CAPT. SCOTT
Go on alone. It's what I want. . . .

FLEMING
But how. . . .

CAPT. SCOTT
I'll last, I'll last. . . . You will have enough time
to send them for me when you reach the inlet.
Go on! Perhaps you'll even meet our men
along the way. I want you to—go on. . . . I
demand it. . . .

FLEMING
Yes, then I shall go, I think. . . .

CAPT. SCOTT
Go on. . . . What will you take along?

FLEMING
The sled
I do not need. . . . I'll only take these skis, and
a stick. . . .

CAPT. SCOTT
No, wait—you take another pair. . . .
It seems to me the heel strap on that ski
is weak. . . .
Farewell. . . . Give me your hand. . . . If you—
no, never mind. . . .

FLEMING
My compass. . . . Damn, it's broken. . . .

CAPT. SCOTT

Here's mine—you take it. . . .

FLEMING

Right. . . .

I guess I'm ready. . . .

All right. Good-bye, Chief. I'll be coming back
with help. No later than tomorrow night. . . .
Be careful not to fall asleep. . . .

CAPT. SCOTT

Farewell. . . . *(Fleming leaves.)*
Yes, he will make it. . . . It's twelve miles. . . . Besides,
the blizzard's dying down. . . . *(pause)*

I need to pray. . . .

My diary—here it is, my humble, faithful
prayer book. . . . Think I'll start in the middle. . . . *(reads)* "Fifteenth
November: moon is blazing like a bonfire;
and Venus seems a little Japanese
lantern. . . ." *(turns page)*

"Bravo for Kingsley. Always looks like
he's playing—sturdy and light-footed. . . . Problems
with our poor dogs: Gypsy's gone blind, and Grouse
has vanished: fell into a seal hole, I
imagine. . . ."

"Christmas Eve: today the sky was
lit up by an aurora borealis. . . ." *(turns page)*
"Eighth February: the Pole. Norwegian flag
is sticking from the snow. . . . We have been beaten.
I'm very sorry for my loyal companions.
And now we must go back." *(turns page)* "Eighteenth of March:
we're straying. Sleds keep getting stuck. And Kingsley
is going downhill." "The twentieth: the last of
the cocoa and meat powder. . . . Johnson's feet

aren't well. He's very cheerful, very lucid.
We still go on discussing, he and I,
what we'll do afterwards, on our return."
Well, . . . Now I must add only that—too bad
the pencil's broken. . . .

                     I suppose it is
the most appropriate ending. . . .

                            Lord, I'm ready.
My life, just like the needle of a compass,
has quivered and has pointed to the Pole—and
Thou art that Pole. . . .

                My skis have left their tracks
upon your boundless snows. There's nothing else.
That's all there is. *(pause)*

               And in a city park,
back home in London, with some toy or other,
all bathed in sunshine, and with naked knees. . . .
They'll tell him later on. . . . *(pause)*

                   Everything's quiet.
I picture Fleming on the vast, smooth plain—
he walks and walks, moving his skis ahead
so steadily—one, two . . . he's disappearing. . . .
And I'm no longer hungry. . . . Such great weakness,
such quietude is rippling through my body. . . . *(pause)*
It's probably delirium. . . . I hear. . . .
I hear. . . . Can it really be possible?
They've found us, here they come . . . our men . . . our men. . . .
Keep calm, Captain, keep calm. . . . No, it is not
delirium, not the wind. I clearly hear
snow creaking, movement, steps upon the snow.
Keep calm . . . must rise . . . must meet them. . . . Who is there?

FLEMING
It's Fleming. . . .

CAPT. SCOTT

                  Ah, the blizzard has died down —
hasn't it? . . .

FLEMING

            Yes, it's cleared up. The wind has stopped. *(sits down)*
The outside of our tent is all aglitter,
powdered with snow. . . .

CAPT. SCOTT

                    Say, do you have a knife?
My pencil's broken. Thanks, this will do fine.
I have to make an entry that you're back.

FLEMING

And you can add that Johnson isn't.

CAPT. SCOTT

                          It's
one and the same. . . .
(pause)

FLEMING

            Our tent will not be hard
to notice, it shines so. . . .
               Oh, by the way,
about Johnson: I came across his body.
He'd dug into the snow, face down, his hood
thrown back. . . .

CAPT. SCOTT

           It seems a pity, but I do
not think I can write more. . . . Now, listen — can

you tell me for what reason you came back. . . .

FLEMING
I simply couldn't help it. . . . He was lying
so well. His death had been so comfortable.
And now I shall remain here. . . .

CAPT. SCOTT
Fleming, you
remember how, as children, we would read
about Sinbad's adventures — you remember?

FLEMING
I do, yes.

CAPT. SCOTT
People are fond of fables, aren't they?
Thus, you and I, alone, amid the snows,
so far away. . . . I think that England. . . .

CURTAIN

The Grand-dad

DRAMA IN ONE ACT

INTRODUCTORY NOTE

The Grand-dad (Dédushka) was completed on 30 June 1923 at the Domaine de Beaulieu. It was published in *Rul'* in Berlin on 14 October of the same year. The English translation is based on a collation of the published text and two almost identical handwritten versions recorded by Nabokov's mother in her albums. What few discrepancies and lapses there were generally had resulted from oversights in copying.

CAST OF CHARACTERS

Wife
Husband
Passerby (de Mérival)
Juliette
Grand-dad

The action takes place in 1816 in France, in the house of a well-off peasant family. A spacious room, with windows giving on a garden. Slanting rain. Enter the owners and a stranger — a passerby.

WIFE

                        . . . Come in. Our living room
is over here. . . .

HUSBAND

                 . . . One moment — we'll have wine
for you. *(to his daughter)*
                   Juliette, run to the cellar, quickly!

PASSERBY
(looking around)
How cozy it is here. . . .

HUSBAND

                      . . . Be seated, please —
here. . . .

PASSERBY

    Bright. . . . And neat. . . . A carved chest in the corner,
a clock up on the wall, its dial adorned
with cornflowers. . . .

WIFE

                Aren't you soaked?

PASSERBY

                           Oh, not at all —
I ducked under a roof in time. A real
downpour! You're certain it's no trouble? May I
wait till it stops? As soon as it is over . . .

HUSBAND
Oh, it's our pleasure. . . .

WIFE

                Are you from nearby?

PASSERBY
A traveler. . . . I've recently returned from
abroad. I'm staying at my brother's castle —
de Mérival. . . . Just a short way from here . . .

HUSBAND
Yes, yes, we know it. . . .
(to his daughter, who has come in with the wine)
              Put it here, Juliette.
There. Drink, good sir. It's sunshine in a glass. . . .

PASSERBY
(clinking glasses)

Your health. . . . Ah, what a fine bouquet! And what
a comely daughter you have too. . . . Juliette,
my sweet, where is your Romeo?

WIFE
(laughing)
What is
a "Romeo"?

PASSERBY
Oh . . . Never mind — one day
she'll learn herself. . . .

JULIETTE
Have you seen Grand-dad yet, sir?

PASSERBY
Not yet.

JULIETTE
He's nice. . . .

HUSBAND
(to Wife)
Say, by the way, where is he?

WIFE
Asleep inside his room, smacking his lips
just like a little child. . . .

PASSERBY
And your grand-dad —
he's very old?

HUSBAND

              Near seventy, I reckon . . .
we do not know. . . .

WIFE

                   He's not our kin, you see:
it was our own idea to call him that.

JULIETTE
He's gentle. . . .

PASSERBY

               But who is he?

HUSBAND

                         That's exactly
the point—we haven't the least idea. . . . One day
last spring an oldster turned up in the village,
and it was clear he came from a great distance.
He had no recollection of his name,
and smiled a timid smile at all our questions.
It was Juliette who brought him to the house.
We gave the old man food, we gave him drink;
he cooed with pleasure, licked his chops, eyes narrowed,
squeezed at my hand, with an enraptured smile,
but made no sense at all; must be his mind
was growing bald. . . . We kept him here with us—
it was Juliette who talked us into it. . . .
He must be coddled, though . . . his tooth is sweet,
and he's been costing us a pretty penny.

WIFE
Oh, stop it, dear . . . the sweet old man. . . .

HUSBAND

                                     I meant
no harm. . . . It was just idle chatter. . . . Drink, sir!

PASSERBY

I'm drinking, thanks. . . . Although it's almost time
for me to go. . . . What rain! It will breathe life
into your land.

HUSBAND

                    Thank heavens. Only this
is just a joke, not rain. There, look—the sun's
beginning to peek through already. . . . No. . . .

PASSERBY

Look at that lovely golden smoke!

HUSBAND

                         See—you, sir,
can marvel at it, but what about us?
We *are* the land. . . . And our thoughts are the land's
own thoughts. . . . We do not need to look, but sense
the swelling of the seed within the furrow,
the fruit becoming plump. . . . When, from the heat,
the earth begins to parch and crack, so, too,
the skin upon our palms starts cracking, sir.
And, if it rains, we listen with alarm,
and inwardly we pray: "Noise, blessed noise,
be not transformed to hammering of hail!" . . .
And if that ricocheting clatter should
begin resounding on our windowsills,
it's then—then that we plug our ears, and bury
our faces in our pillows, just like cowards

who hear a distant fusillade! Our worries
are many. . . . As when, lately, in the pear tree,
a worm appeared—a monstrous, warty worm,
a green-hued devil! Or when aphids, like
a clammy rash, will coat a youthful vine. . . .
And so it goes.

PASSERBY

                Yet what a sense of pride
for you, what joy it must be to receive
the ruddy, aromatic thank-you's that
your trees give to you!

WIFE

                Grand-dad, too, awaits
assiduously some kind of revelation,
pressing his ear first to the bark, then to
a petal. . . . He believes, it seems to me,
that dead men's souls live on in lilies, or
in cherry trees.

PASSERBY

                I wouldn't mind a chat
with him—I'm fond of gentle simpletons
like that. . . .

WIFE

                I look and look at you but I
just cannot figure out your age. You don't seem
too young, and yet there's something. . . . I don't know. . . .

PASSERBY

Dear lady, I'm in my sixth decade.

HUSBAND

                         Then
you've lived a life of peace—there's not a wrinkle
upon your brow. . . .

PASSERBY

                    Of peace, you say! *(laughs)* If I
wrote it all down. . . . Sometimes I, even, cannot
believe my past! My head spins from it as . . .
as it does from your wine. I've drained the cup
of life in such enormous draughts, such draughts. . . .
And then there were times, too, when death would nudge
my elbow. . . . Well, perhaps you'd like to hear
the tale of how, the summer of the year
seventeen ninety-two, in Lyon, Monsieur
de Mérival—aristocrat, and traitor,
so on, so forth—was saved right from the scaffold
of the guillotine?

WIFE

                    We're listening, tell
us. . . .

PASSERBY

          I was twenty that tempestuous year.
And the tribunal's thunder had condemned me
to death—perhaps it was my powdered hair,
or else, perhaps, the noble particle
before my name—who knows: the merest trifle
meant execution then. . . . That very night I
was to appear, by torchlight, at the scaffold.
The executioner was nimble, by
the way, and diligent: an artist, not

an axman. He was always emulating
his Paris cousin, the renowned Sanson:
he had procured the same kind of small tumbrel
and, when he'd lopped a head off, he would hold
it by the hair and swing it the same way. . . .
And so he carts me off. Darkness had fallen,
along black streets the windows came alight,
and street lamps too. I sat, back to the wind,
inside the shaky cart, clutching the side rails
with hands numb from the cold—and I was thinking . . .
of what?—of various trivial details mostly:
that I had left without a handkerchief,
or that my executioner companion
looked like a dignified physician. . . . Soon we
arrived. A final turning, and before us
there opened up the square's expanse. . . . Its center
was ominously lit. . . . And it was then,
as, with a kind of guilty courtesy,
the executioner helped me descend,
and I realized the journey's end had come—
that was the moment terror seized my throat. . . .
Lugubrious hallooing midst the crowd—
derisive, maybe, too (I couldn't hear)—
the horses' moving croups, the lances, wind,
the smell of burning torches—all of this
passed like a dream, and I saw but one thing,
just one: there, there, up in the murky sky,
like a steel wing, the heavy oblique blade
between two uprights hung, ready to fall. . . .
Its edge, catching a transient gleam, appeared
to be already glistening with blood!
To rumblings from the distant crowd, I started
to ascend the scaffold, and each step
would make a different creak. In silence they

removed my camisole, and slashed my shirt
down to my scapulae. . . . The board seemed a
raised drawbridge: to it I'd be lashed, I knew,
the bridge would drop, I'd swing face down, and then,
between the posts the wooden collar would
slam tight on me, and then — yes, only then —
death, with an instant crash, would plummet down.
It grew impossible for me to swallow,
my nape was racked by a presentient pain,
my temples thundered and my chest was bursting,
tensed with the palpitation and the pounding —
but, I believe, I outwardly seemed calm. . . .

WIFE

Oh, I'd be screaming, lunging — my entreaties
for mercy would be heard, and I'd . . . But then —
then how did *you* escape?

PASSERBY

                    A miracle. . . .
So — I was standing on the scaffold. They
had not yet bound my hands. My shoulders felt
the frigid wind. The executioner was
unraveling some kind of rope. Just then —
a cry of "fire!" and instantly flames shot
up from behind the rail; I and the headsman
were swaying, struggling on the platform's edge. . . .
A crackling — and the heat breathed on my face,
the hand that had been clutching me relaxed,
I fell somewhere, knocked someone down, I dove,
I slid, amid torrents of smoke, into
a storm of rearing steeds and running people —
"Fire! Fire!" the cry vibrated over and over,
choking with sobs of joy, with boundless bliss!

But I was far away by then! Just once
I looked back, on the run, and saw the crimson
smoke billowing into a vault of black,
the uprights bursting into flames themselves,
the blade come crashing down, set free by fire!

WIFE
How dreadful! . . .

HUSBAND
                          Yes, when you've seen death you don't
forget. . . . One time some thieves got in the garden.
The night, the darkness, fright. . . . I got my gun off
its hook—

PASSERBY
(interrupting, lost in thought)
                          —Thus I escaped, and suddenly
it seemed my eyes were opened: I'd been awkward,
unfeeling, absent-minded, had not fully
appreciated life, the colored specks of
our precious life—but, having seen so close
that pair of upright posts, that narrow gate
to nonexistence, and those gleams, that gloom. . . .
Amid the whistle of sea winds I fled
from France, and kept avoiding France so long
as over her the icy Robespierre
loomed like a greenish incubus, so long
as dusty armies marched into the gunfire
spurred by the Corsican's gray gaze and forelock.
But life was hard for me in foreign countries.
In dank and melancholy London I
gave lessons in the science of duelling. I
sojourned in Russia, playing the fiddle at

an opulent barbarian's abode. . . .
In Turkey and in Greece I wandered then,
and in enchanting Italy I starved.
The sights I saw were many; I became
a deckhand, then a chef, a barber, a tailor,
then just a simple tramp. Yet, to this day
I thank the Lord with every passing hour
for all the hardships that I came to know—
and for the rustle of the roadside corn,
the rustle and the warming breath of all
the human souls that have passed close to me.

HUSBAND
Of all, sir, all of them? But you forget
the soul belonging to that flashy craftsman
whom you encountered that day on the scaffold.

PASSERBY
Oh, no—through him the world revealed itself
to me. He was, unwittingly, the key.

HUSBAND
No, I don't get it. . . . *(rising)* Before supper, I
have chores to do. . . . Our meal is unpretentious . . .
but maybe you'll—

PASSERBY
                    Why not, why not. . . .

HUSBAND
                                        Agreed, then! *(going out)*

PASSERBY
Forgive my talkativeness. . . . I'm afraid

my tale was boring. . . .

WIFE

Goodness, not at all. . . .

PASSERBY

Is that a baby's bonnet you are sewing?

WIFE

(laughs)

That's right. I think I'll need it around Christmas. . . .

PASSERBY

How wonderful. . . .

WIFE

And that's another baby,
there, in the garden. . . .

PASSERBY

(looks out the window)

Oh—your "grand-dad." Splendid
old man. . . . The sun gives him a silvery sheen.
Splendid . . . and there's a certain dreamy air
about his movements, as his fingers slide
along a lily stem, and he is bent
over the flower bed, not picking, just
caressing, all aglow with such a tender
and timid smile. . . .

WIFE

That's true, he loves the lilies—
he fondles them, has conversations with them.

He even has invented names for them —
all names of duchesses, of marquesses. . . .

PASSERBY
How nice for him. . . . Now *he* is one, I'm certain,
who's lived his life in peace — yes, in some village,
away from civil and from other tumults. . . .

WIFE
He's good at doctoring. . . . Knows all about
medicinal herbs. Once, for our daughter —
(Juliette bursts in, laughing boisterously.)

JULIETTE

                        Mother!
Oh, Mother! You'll die laughing!

WIFE

                    What's the matter?

JULIETTE
Grand-dad . . . out there . . . the basket. . . . Oh! *(laughs)*

WIFE

                      Come on,
let's hear it properly. . . .

JULIETTE
              You'll die. . . . See, Mother,
I was just going — I was going through
the garden to pick cherries. . . . Grand-dad sees me,
gets in a crouch, then snatches at my basket —
the new one, the one with the oilcloth lining,

already stained with juice—he snatches it,
and heaves it all the way into the stream. . . .
By now the current's carried it away.

PASSERBY
How very odd. God only knows in what
directions, in his brain, the thoughts make bridges. . . .
Could be that . . . no. *(laughs)* Sometimes I tend myself
to strange associations. . . . Like that basket,
its oilcloth lining with the cherries' juice
incarnadined—it brings to mind. . . . Good God,
what chilling nonsense! You'll permit me not
to finish. . . .

WIFE
(not listening)
              What's got into him? Your father
will be angry. Twenty sous, that basket. *(leaves with her daughter)*

PASSERBY
(looking out the window)
They're bringing him. . . . It's funny how he sulks,
the old man. . . . Just like an offended child. . . .

WIFE
(They return with Grand-dad.)
Here, Grand-dad, we've a guest. . . . Just look at him. . . .

GRAND-DAD
I do not want that basket here. There must
not be such baskets. . . .

WIFE
              It's all right, my dear. . . .

It isn't there. It's gone. It's gone for good.
Come on, calm down. . . . Good sir, perhaps you could
distract him for a while. . . . I have to go
and start preparing supper. . . .

GRAND-DAD

                    Who is this?
No, I don't want . . .

WIFE
(in the doorway)

                    But that's our guest. He's kind.
Sit down, sit down. What stories he has told us!
About the executioner in Lyon,
the guillotine, the fire! It's fascinating.
Tell it again, sir. *(leaves with her daughter)*

GRAND-DAD

                    What? What was that she
just said? That's strange. . . . The executioner,
the fire . . .

PASSERBY
(aside)

                    There, now he's frightened. Silly woman —
why did she ever have to tell him that?
(full voice)
It was a joke, Grand-dad. . . . Tell me instead,
what do you chat about out there with flowers,
with trees? . . . Why do you look at me like that?

GRAND-DAD
(staring at him intently)
Where are you from?

PASSERBY

Oh . . . simply passing by . . .

GRAND-DAD

Wait,
just wait, don't go away, I'll be right back. *(goes out)*

PASSERBY
(pacing the room)
Odd character! Either he's had a fright
or he's remembered something. . . . I've an eerie,
a troubled feeling—I don't understand. . . .
The wine they have here must be strong. Tra-ram,
tra-ra. . . . *(sings)* What's wrong with me? I seem to feel
some kind of vague oppression. . . . Ugh! How stupid. . . .

GRAND-DAD
(enters)
And here I am. . . . I'm back. . . .

PASSERBY

Hello, hello. . . .
(aside)
Look how he's grown all nice and cheery now.

GRAND-DAD
(shifting from foot to foot, hands behind his back)
Here's where I live. Right in this house. I like
it here. For instance, over there, look at
that wardrobe. . . .

PASSERBY

Beautiful. . . .

GRAND-DAD

                        You know, that's an
enchanted wardrobe. . . . Oh, the things, the things that
go on inside! You see that chink, that keyhole?
Peek through it . . . Eh?

PASSERBY

                    Enchanted? I believe you. . . .
It's beautiful. . . . You didn't tell me, though,
about the lilies, and your talks with them.

GRAND-DAD
Peek through the chink. . . .

PASSERBY

                        I can see fine from here. . . .

GRAND-DAD
No, take a closer look.

PASSERBY

                        I can't — that table
is in the way. . . .

GRAND-DAD

                    Lie on the table — lie
on it, face down. . . .

PASSERBY

                    Oh, come, it isn't worth it.

GRAND-DAD
Don't want to do it?

PASSERBY

                  ... Look, look at that sunshine!
And your whole garden sparkling. . . .

GRAND-DAD

                          You don't want to?
A shame. . . . A real shame. It would be much
more comfortable.

PASSERBY

             More comfortable? For what?

GRAND-DAD

For what? *(swings with the axe he has been holding behind
his back)*

PASSERBY

       Hold on there! Stop!
(They struggle.)

GRAND-DAD

                 No. . . . Wait. . . . You must
not interfere. . . . It is decreed. . . . My duty. . . .

PASSERBY

(knocks him down)
Enough!
         There—there, that's it—that madness. . . . God! . . .
I didn't expect it. . . . He was mumbling, purring—
then suddenly . . .
           What *is* this? I think it
already happened once. . . . Or did I dream it?
The same way, just the same, I struggled. . . . Up!

Enough, get up! Reply! . . . Look how he stares,
and stares. . . . Look at those fingers, naked, blunt. . . .
I've seen them once before, I know! You'll answer,
you will! . . . That stare. . . . *(bends over the prostrate figure)*
                    No, he will tell me nothing.

JULIETTE
(in the doorway)
What have you done to Grand-dad? . . .

PASSERBY
                                        Juliette . . .
You'd . . . better go.

JULIETTE
                    What have you done. . . .

CURTAIN

ESSAYS

INTRODUCTION

The lectures "The Tragedy of Tragedy" and "Playwriting" were composed for a course on drama that Nabokov gave at Stanford during the summer of 1941. We had arrived in America in May of 1940; except for some brief guest appearances, this was Father's first lecturing engagement at an American university. The Stanford course also included a discussion of some American plays, a survey of Soviet theatre, and an analysis of commentary on drama by several American critics.

The two lectures presented here have been selected to accompany Nabokov's plays because they embody, in concentrated form, many of his principal guidelines for writing, reading, and performing plays. The reader is urged to bear in mind, however, that, later in life, Father might have expressed certain thoughts differently.

The lectures were partly in typescript and partly in manuscript, replete with Nabokov's corrections, additions, deletions, occasional slips of the pen, and references to previous and subsequent installments of the course. I have limited myself to what editing seemed necessary for the presentation of the lectures in essay form. If Nabokov had been alive, he might perhaps have performed more radical surgery. He might also have added that the gruesome throes of realistic suicide he finds unacceptable onstage (in "The Tragedy of Tragedy") are now everyday fare on kiddies' TV, while "adult" entertainment has long since outdone all the goriness of the Grand Guignol. He might have observed that the aberrations of theatrical method wherein the illusion of a barrier between stage and audience is shattered—a phenomenon he considered "freakish"—are now commonplace: actors wander and mix; the audience is invited to participate; it is then applauded by the players in a curious reversal of roles made chic by Soviet performers ordered to emulate the mise-en-scène of party congresses; and the term "happening" has already managed to grow obsolescent. He might have commented that the quest for originality for its own sake has led to ludicrous excesses and things have taken their helter-skelter course in random theatre as they have in random music and in random painting.

Yet Nabokov's own plays demonstrate that it is possible to respect the rules of drama and still be original, just as one can write original poetry without neglecting the basic requirements of prosody, or play brilliant tennis, to paraphrase T. S. Eliot, without taking down the net.

There were those who considered Father's professorial persona odd and vaguely improper. Not only was he unsympathetic to the intrusion of administrative matters on the academic and to the use of valuable time for jovial participation in campus life, but he lectured from carefully composed texts instead of chattily extemporizing. "All of a sudden," says Nabokov, "I realized that I was totally incapable of public speaking. I decided to write in advance a good hundred lectures. . . . Thanks to this method I never fumbled, and the auditorium received the pure product of my knowledge."[1]

I suspect that, since the day when the various Nabokov lectures, resurrected from notes made more than three decades before, began to appear in print, at least some of those objectors have realized that Father's single-mindedness and meticulous preparation had their advantages.

There were even those who resented Nabokov's being allowed to teach at all, lest the bastions of academic mediocrity be imperiled. Which brings to mind Roman Jakobson's uneasy quip when Nabokov was being considered for a permanent position at Harvard: "Are we next to invite an elephant to be professor of zoology?" If the elephant happens also to be a brilliant scholar and (as his former Cornell colleague David Daiches put it) a lecturer whom everyone found "irresistible," why not? Anyway, time has put things in perspective: those who (attentively) attended Nabokov's lectures will not soon forget them. Those who missed them regret it but have the published versions to enjoy. As for Professor Jakobson (and I intend no malice), I have been racking my brain but cannot, for the life of me, recall whether or not I took a course of his at some point during my four years at Harvard. Perhaps what I need is the memory of an elephant.

DMITRI NABOKOV

[1]*Apostrophes,* French television, 1975. © Article 3b Trust Under the Will of Vladimir Nabokov.

Playwriting

The one and only stage convention that I accept may be formulated in the following way: the people you see or hear can under no circumstances see or hear you. This convention is at the same time a unique feature of the dramatic art: under no circumstances of human life can the most secret watcher or eavesdropper be absolutely immune to the possibility of being found out by those he is spying upon, not other people in particular, but the world as a whole. A closer analogy is the relation between an individual and outside nature; this, however, leads to a philosophical idea which I shall refer to at the end of this lecture. A play is an ideal conspiracy, because, even though it is absolutely exposed to our view, we are as powerless to influence the course of action as the stage inhabitants are to see us, while influencing our inner selves with almost superhuman ease. We have thus the paradox of an invisible world of free spirits (ourselves) watching uncontrollable but earthbound proceedings, which—a compensation—are endowed with the power of exactly that spiritual intervention which we invisible watchers paradoxically lack. Sight and hearing but no intervention on one side and spiritual intervention but no sight or hearing on the other are the main features of the beautifully balanced and perfectly fair division drawn by the line of footlights. It may be proved further that this convention is a natural rule of the theatre and that when there is any freakish attempt to break it, then either the breaking is only a delusion, or the play stops being a play. That is why I call ridiculous the attempts of the Soviet theatre to have the spectators join in the play. This is connected with the assumption that the players themselves are spectators and, indeed, we can easily imagine inexperienced actors under slapdash management in the dumb parts of attendants just as engrossed in watching the performance of the great actor in the major part as we, ordinary spectators, are. But, besides the danger of letting even the least important actor remain *outside* the play, there exists one inescapable law, a law (laid down by that genius of the stage, Stanislavsky) that invalidates all reasoning deriving from the delusion that the footlights are not as definite a separation between spectator and player as our main stage convention implies. Roughly speaking, this law is that, provided he does not annoy his neighbors, the spectator is perfectly free to do whatever he pleases, to yawn or laugh, or to arrive late, or to leave his place if he is bored with the play or has business elsewhere; but the man on the stage, however inactive and mute he is, is absolutely bound by the conspiracy of the stage and by its main convention: that is, he may *not* wander back into the wings for a drink or a chat, nor may he indulge in any physical exuberance that would clash with the idea of his part. And, vice-versa, if we imagine some playwright or manager, brimming over with those collectivist and mass-loving notions that are a blight in regard to all art, making the spectators play, too (as a crowd, for instance, reacting to certain doings or speeches; even going so far as to hand round, for instance, printed words that the spectators must say aloud, or just leaving these words to our own discretion; turning the stage loose into the house and having the regular actors mingle with the audience, etc.), such a method, apart from the ever-lurking possibility of the play's being wrecked by the local wit or fatally suffering from the unpreparedness of impromptu actors, is an utter delusion to boot, because the spectator remains perfectly free to refuse to participate and may leave the theatre if he does not care for such fooling. In the case of his being forced to act because the play refers to the Perfect State and is running in the governmental theatre of a country ruled by a dictator, the theatre in such case is merely a barbarous ceremony or a Sunday-school class for the teaching of police regulation—or again, what goes on in theatre is the same as goes on in the dictator's country, public life being the constant and universal acting in the dreadful farce composed by a stage-minded Father of the People.

So far I have dwelt chiefly on the spectator's side of the question: awareness and nonintervention. But cannot one imagine the players, in accordance with a dramatist's whim or thoroughly worn-out idea, actually seeing the public and talking to it from the stage? In other words, I am trying to find whether there is really no loophole in what I take to be the essential formula, the essential and only convention of the stage. I remember, in fact, several plays where this trick has been used, but the all-important thing is that, when the player stalks up to the footlights and addresses himself to the audience with a supposed explanation or an ardent plea, this audience is not the actual audience before him, but an audience imagined by the playwright, that is, something which is still *on the stage,* a theatrical illusion which is the more intensified the more naturally and casually such an appeal is made. In other words, the line that a character cannot cross without interrupting the play is this abstract conception that the author has of an audience; as soon as he sees it as a pink collection of familiar faces the play stops being a play. To give an instance, my grandfather, my mother's father, an exceedingly eccentric Russian who got the idea of having a private theatre in his house and hiring the very greatest performers of his time to entertain for him and his friends, was on a friendly footing with most of the actors of the Russian stage and a regular theatregoer. One night, at one of the St. Petersburg theatres, the famous Varlamov was impersonating someone having tea on a terrace and conversing the while with passersby who were invisible to the spectators. The part bored Varlamov, and that night he brightened it up with certain harmless inventions of his own. Then at one point he turned in the direction of my grandfather, whom he espied in the front row, and remarked, quite naturally, as if speaking to the imaginary passersby: "By the way, Ivan Vasilich, I'm afraid I shall be unable to have luncheon with you tomorrow." And just because Varlamov was such a perfect magician and managed to fit these words so naturally into his scene, it did not occur to my grandfather that his friend was really and truly canceling an appointment; in other words, the power of the stage is such, that even if, as sometimes has happened, an actor in the middle of his performance falls in a dead faint or, owing to a blunder, a stagehand is trapped among the characters when the curtain goes up, it will take the spectator much longer to realize the accident or the mistake than if anything out of the ordinary happens in the house. Destroy the spell and you kill the play.

My theme being the writing of plays and not the staging of plays, I shall not develop further what really would lead me into discussing the psychology of acting. I am merely concerned, let me repeat, with settling the problem of one convention, so as to fiercely criticize and demolish all the other minor ones that infect plays. I will prove, I hope, that continuously yielding to them is slowly but surely killing playwriting as an art, and that there is no real difficulty in getting rid of them forever, even if it entails inventing new means, which in their turn will become traditional conventions with time, to be dismissed again when they stiffen and hamper and imperil dramatic art. A play limited by my major formula may be compared to a clock; but when it comes out hobnobbing with the audience, it becomes a wound-up top, which bumps into something, screeches, rolls on its side and is dead. Please note, too, that the formula holds not only when you see a play performed, but also when you read it in a book. And here I come to a very important point. There exists an old fallacy according to which some plays are meant to be seen, others to be read. True, there are two sorts of plays: verb plays and adjective plays, plain plays of action and florid plays of characterization — but apart from such a classification being merely a superficial convenience, a fine play of either type is equally delightful on the stage and at home. The only thing is that a type of play where poetry, symbolism, description, lengthy monologues tend to hamper its dramatic action ceases in its extreme form to be a play at all, becoming a long poem or full-dress speech — so that the question whether it is better read than seen does not arise, because it is simply not a play. But, within certain limits, an adjective play is no worse on the stage than a verb play, though the best plays are generally a combination of both action and poetry.

For the time being, pending further explanation, we may assume that a play can be anything it likes, static or tit-for-tatic, round or fancy-shaped, nimble or stately, provided it is a good play.

We must draw a definite line between the author's gift and the theatre's contribution. I am speaking only of the former and refer to the latter insofar as the author has imagined it. It is quite clear that as bad direction or a bad cast may ruin the best play, the theatre may turn everything into a couple of hours of fugitive glamour. A nonsense rhyme may be staged by a director or actor of genius and a mere pun may be turned into a splendid show owing to the sets of a gifted painter. But all this has nothing to do with the dramatist's task; it may clarify and bring to life his suggestions, it can even make a bad play look—and only look—like a good one; but the merits of the play as disclosed by the printed word are what they are, not more, not less. In fact, I cannot think of a single fine drama that is not a pleasure both to see and read, though, to be sure, a certain part of footlight-pleasure is not the same as the corresponding part of reading-lamp pleasure, the one being in that part *sensual* (good show, fine acting), the other being in the corresponding part *purely imaginative* (which is compensated by the fact that any definite incarnation is always a limitation of possibilities). But the main and most important part of the pleasure is exactly the same in both cases. It is the delight in harmony, artistic truth, fascinating surprises, and the deep satisfaction at being surprised—and, mind you, the surprise is always there even if you have seen the play and read the book many times. For perfect pleasure the stage must not be too bookish and the book not too stagy. You will note that complicated setting is generally described (with very minute details and at great length) in the pages of the worst plays (Shaw's excepted) and, vice versa, that very good plays are rather indifferent to the setting. Such ponderous descriptions of paraphernalia, generally allied with a prefaced description of the characters and with a whole string of qualifying adverbs in italics directing every speech in the play, are, more often than not, the result of an author's feeling that his play does not contain all it is meant to contain — and so off he goes in a pathetic and long-winded attempt to strengthen matters by decorative addition. More rarely, such superfluous ornamentation is dictated by the strong-willed author's desire to have the play staged and acted exactly as he intended — but even in this case the method is highly irritating.

We are now ready, as we see the curtain rise, or as we open the book, to examine the structure of a play itself. But we must be quite clear on one point. Henceforth, once the initial convention is accepted — spiritual awareness and physical non-intervention on our side, physical non-awareness and significant intervention on the part of the play — all others will be ruled out.

In conclusion, let me repeat in slightly different words — now that I have defined the general idea — repeat the primary axiom of drama. If, as I believe it to be, the only acceptable dualism is the unbridgeable division between ego and non-ego, then we can say that the theatre is a good illustration of this philosophical fatality. My initial formula referring to the spectators and the drama onstage may be expressed thus: the first is aware of the second but has no power over it; the second is unaware of the first, but has the power of moving it. Broadly speaking, this is very near to what happens in the mutual relations between myself and the world I see, and this too is not merely a formula of existence, but also a necessary convention without which neither I nor the world could exist. I have then examined certain consequences of the formula convention of the theatre and found that neither the stage overflowing into the audience nor the audience dictating its will to the stage can break this convention without destroying the essential idea of the drama. And here again the concept can be likened, on a higher level, to the philosophy of existence by saying that in life, too, any attempt at tampering with the world or any attempt by the world to tamper with me is extremely risky business even if in both cases the best intentions are implied. And finally I have spoken of how reading a play and seeing a play correspond to living one's life and dreaming of one's life, of how both experiences afford the same pleasure, if in somewhat different ways.

The Tragedy
of Tragedy

Discussion of the technique of modern tragedy means to me
a grim examination of something which may be termed the
tragedy of the art of tragedy. The bitterness with which I
view the plight of playwriting does not really imply that all
is lost and that the contemporary theatre may be dismissed
with that rather primitive gesture—a shrug of the shoulders.
But what I do mean is that unless something is done by
somebody, and done soon, playwriting will cease to be the
subject of any discussion dealing with literary values. The
drama will be completely taken over by showmanship, completely absorbed by that other art, the art of staging and acting,
a great art to be sure which I love ardently but which is as
remote from the writer's essential business as any other art:
painting, or music, or dancing. Thus, a play will be created
by the management, the actors, the stagehands—and a
couple of meek scriptwriters whom nobody heeds; it will be
based on collaboration, and collaboration will certainly
never produce anything as permanent as can be the work of
one man because however much talent the collaborators may
individually possess the final result will unavoidably be a
compromise between talents, a certain average, a trimming

and clipping, a rational number distilled out of the fusion of irrational ones. This complete transferring of everything connected with the drama into hands which, according to my firm belief, are meant to receive the ripe fruit (the final result of one man's labor), is a rather dismal prospect, but it may be the logical outcome of the conflict which has been tearing the drama, and especially tragedy, for several centuries.

First of all let us attempt to define what we mean by "tragedy." As used in everyday speech, the term is so closely allied to the idea of destiny as to be almost synonymous with it — at least when the presupposed destiny is not one that we would be inclined to relish. In this sense, tragedy without a background of fate is hardly perceptible to the ordinary observer. If, say, a person goes out and kills another person, of more or less the same sex, just because he happened to be that day in a more or less killing mood, there is no tragedy or, more exactly, the murderer in this case is not a tragic character. He will tell the police that everything went sort of black and experts will be invited to measure his sanity — that will be all. But if a perfectly respectable man is slowly but inexorably (and by the way the "slowly" and the "inexorably" are so used to being together that the "but" between them ought to be replaced by the wedding ring of an "and") driven to murder by the creep and crawl of circumstance, or by a long-repressed passion, or by anything that has long been working at undermining his will, by things, in short, against which he has been hopelessly and perhaps nobly struggling — then, whatever his crime, we see in him a tragic figure. Or again: you happen to meet socially a person of perfectly normal aspect, good-natured although a little seedy, pleasant though something of a bore, a trifle foolish, perhaps, but not more so than anybody else, a character to whom you would never dream of applying the adjective "tragic"; then you learn that this person several years ago had been placed by force of circumstance at the head of some great revolution in a remote, almost legendary country, and that a new force of circumstance had soon banished him to your part of the world where he lingers on as the mere ghost of his past glory. Immediately, the very things about the man that had just seemed to you humdrum (indeed, the very normality of his aspect) now strike you as the very features of tragedy. King Lear, Nuncle Lear, is even more tragic when he potters about the place than when he actually kills the prison guard who was a-hanging his daughter.

So what is the result of our little inquest into the popular meaning of "tragedy"? The result is that we find the term "tragedy" not only synonymous with fate, but also synonymous with our knowledge of another man's slow and inexorable fate. Our next step must be to find what is meant by "fate."

From the two intentionally vague examples that I have selected, one thing, however, may be clearly deduced. What we learn of another man's fate is far more than he knows himself. In fact, if he knows himself to be a tragic figure and acts accordingly, we cease to be interested in him. Our knowledge of his fate is not objective knowledge. Our imagination breeds monsters which the subject of our sympathy may never have seen. He may have been confronted with other terrors, other sleepless nights, other heartbreaking incidents of which we know nothing. The line of destiny which *ex post facto* seems so clear to us may have been in reality a wild scallop interwoven with other wild scallops of fate or fates. This or that social or economic background which, if we are Marxist-minded, seems to have played such an imporant part in the subject's life may have had nothing to do with it in this or that particular case, although it does seem to explain everything so neatly.

Consequently, all we possess in regard to our own judgment of another man's tragic fate is a handful of facts most of which the man would repudiate; but to this is added what our imagination supplies, and this imagination of ours is regulated by a sound logic, and this sound logic of ours is so hypnotized by the conventionally accepted rules of cause and effect that it will invent a cause and modify an effect rather than have none at all.

And now observe what has happened. Gossiping around a man's fate has automatically led us to construct a stage tragedy, partly because we have seen so many of them at the theatre or at the other place of entertainment, but mainly because we cling to the same old iron bars of determinism which have imprisoned the spirit of playwriting for years and years. And this is where lies the tragedy of tragedy.

Consider the following curious position: on one hand a written tragedy belongs to creative literature although at the same time it clings to old rules, to dead traditions which other forms of literature enjoy breaking, finding in this process perfect liberty, a liberty without which no art can thrive; and, on the other hand, a written tragedy belongs also to the stage — and here too the theatre positively revels in the freedom of fanciful sets and in the genius of individual acting. The highest achievements in poetry, prose, painting, showmanship are characterized by the irrational and illogical, by that spirit of free will that snaps its rainbow fingers in the face of smug causality. But where is the corresponding development in drama? What masterpieces can we name except a few dream-tragedies resplendent with genius, such as *King Lear* or *Hamlet*, Gogol's *Inspector*, and perhaps one or two Ibsen plays (these last with reservations), what masterpieces can we name that might be compared to the numberless glories of novels and short stories and verse produced during these last three or four centuries? What plays, to put it bluntly, are ever re-read?

The most popular plays of yesterday are on the level of the worst novels of yesterday. The best plays of today are on the level of magazine stories and fat best-sellers. And the highest form of the dramatic art—tragedy—is at its best a clockwork toy made in Greece that little children wind up on the carpet and then follow on all fours.

I referred to Shakespeare's two greatest plays as dream-tragedies, and in the same sense I would have called Gogol's *Revizor* a dream-play, or Flaubert's *Bouvard et Pécuchet* a dream-novel. My definition has certainly nothing to do with that special brand of pretentious "dream-play" which was at one time popular, and which was really regulated by the most wide-awake causality, if not by worse things such as Freudianism. I call *King Lear* or *Hamlet* dream-tragedies because dream-logic, or perhaps better say nightmare-logic, replaces here the elements of dramatic determinism. Incidentally, I want to stress the point that the way Shakespeare is produced in all countries is not Shakespeare at all, but a garbled version flavored with this or that fad which is sometimes amusing as in the Russian theatre and sometimes nauseating as, for instance, in Piscator's trashy concoctions. There is something I am very positive about and that is that Shakespeare must be produced in toto, without a single syllable missing, or not at all. But from the logical, causal, point of view, that is, from the point of view of modern producers, both *Lear* and *Hamlet* are impossibly bad plays, and I dare any contemporary popular theatre to stage them strictly according to the text.

Better scholars than I have discussed the influence of Greek tragedy on Shakespeare. In my time I have read the Greeks in English translation and found them very much weaker than Shakespeare though disclosing his influence here and there. The relays of fire in the *Agamemnon* of Aeschylus o'erleaping the plain, flashing across the lake, rambling up the mountainside, or Iphigenia shedding her crocus-tinctured tunic—these excite me because they remind me of Shakespeare. But I refuse to be touched by the abstract passions and vague emotions of those characters, as eyeless and as armless as that statue which for some reason or other is considered ideally beautiful; and moreover I do not quite see how a direct contact with our emotion can be established by Aeschylus when the profoundest scholars themselves cannot say for sure in what way this or that context points, what exactly we are to guess l ere and what there, and then wind up saying that the removal of the article from this or that word obscures and has in fact made unintelligible the connection and construction of the sentence. Indeed, the main drama seems to take place in these minute and copious footnotes. However, the excitements of inspired grammar are not exactly the emotions which the theatre can greet, and on the other hand what passes muster as Greek tragedy on our stage is so far removed from the original, so influenced by this or that stage version and stage invention, and these in turn are so influenced by the secondary conventions which the primary ones of Greek tragedy had engendered, that it is hard to say what we mean when we praise Aeschylus.

One thing is, however, certain: the idea of logical fate which, unfortunately, we inherited from the ancients has, ever since, been keeping the drama in a kind of concentration camp. Now and then a genius would escape as Shakespeare did more often than not; Ibsen has half-escaped in *Doll's House*, while in his *Borkman* the drama actually leaves the stage and goes up a winding road, up a remote hill—a curious symbol of that urge which genius feels to be free from the shackles of convention. But Ibsen has sinned too: he had spent many years in Scribia, and in this respect the incredibly absurd results to which the conventions of causality can lead are well displayed in the *Pillars of Society.* The plot, as you remember, turns on the idea of two ships, one good and the other bad. One of them, the *Gypsy,* is now in beautiful shape as it lies all ready to sail for America in the shipyard of which the main character is master. The other ship, the *Indian Girl,* is blessed with all the ills that can befall a ship. It is old and rickety, manned by a wild drunken crew, and it is not repaired before its return voyage to America — just carelessly patched up by the overseer (act of sabotage against the new kinds of machinery which lessen the earnings of workers). The main character's brother is supposed to sail to America, and the main character has reasons to wish his brother at the bottom of the sea. Simultaneously, the main character's little son is secretly preparing to run away to sea. Given these circumstances, the author was forced by the goblins of cause and effect to subject everything concerning the ships to the different emotional and physical moves of the characters with a view to achieving the maximum of effect when, simultaneously, both brother and son put out to sea — the brother sailing on the good ship instead of the bad one which, against all rules, knowing it was rotten, the villain allows to sail, and his adored son heading for the bad one, so that he will perish through his father's fault. The moves of the play are exceedingly complicated, and the weather — now stormy, now fair, now again dirty — is adjusted to these various moves, always in such a manner as to give the maximum of suspense without bothering about likelihood. When one follows this "shipyard line" throughout the play, one notices that it forms a pattern which in a very comical way turns out to be specially, and solely, adapted to the needs of the author. The weather is forced to resort to the most eerie dialectical tricks, and, when at the happy ending the ships do sail (without the boy who has been retrieved just in time, and with the brother who at the last moment proved to be not worth killing), the weather suddenly becomes not only fair, but supernaturally fair—and this leads me to one of the most important points in the dismal technique of modern drama.

The weather, as I say, had been feverishly changing throughout the play in accordance with the feverish changes of the plot. Now, when at the end of the play neither of the two ships is meant to sink, the weather turns to fair, and we know—this is my point—we know that the weather will remain metaphysically fair after the curtain has gone down, for ever and ever. This is what I term the positive finality idea. However variable the moves of man and sky may have been during the four acts, they will retain forever that particular move which permeates the very last bit of the last act. This positive-finality idea is a direct consequence of the cause-and-effect idea: the effect is final because we are limited by the prison regulations we have adopted. In what we call "real life" every effect is at the same time the cause of some other effect, so that the classification itself of causality is merely a matter of standpoint. But, though in "real life" we are not able to cut away one limb of life from other branching limbs, we do perform this operation in stage drama, and thus the effect is final, for it is not supposed to contain any new cause that would explode it somewhere beyond the play.

A fine specimen of the positive finality motif is the stage suicide. Here is what happens. The only logical way of leaving the effect of the end of the play quite pure, i.e. without the faintest possibility of any further causal transformation beyond the play, is to have the life of the main character *end* at the same time as the play. This seems perfect. But is it? Let us see how the man can be removed permanently. There are three ways: natural death, murder, and suicide. Now, natural death is ruled out because, however patiently prepared, however many heart attacks the patient endures in the exposition, it is almost impossible for a determinist playwright to convince a determinist audience that he has not been helping the hand of God; the audience will inevitably regard such a natural death as an evasion, an accident, a weak unconvincing end, especially as it must happen rather suddenly, so as not to interfere with the last act by a needless display of agony. I presuppose naturally that the patient has been struggling with fate, that he has sinned, etc. I certainly do not mean that natural death is always unconvincing: it is only the cause-and-effect idea that makes natural death occurring at the right moment look a little too smart. So this first method is excluded.

The second one is murder. Now, murder is all very well at the beginning of a play. It is a very uncomfortable thing to have at its close. The man who has sinned and struggled, etc., is doubtlessly removed. But his murderer remains, and even if we may be plausibly sure that society will pardon him, we are left with the uncomfortable sensation that we do not exactly know how he will feel in the long years following the final curtain; and whether the fact of his having murdered a man, however necessary it might have been, will not influence somehow all his future life, for instance his relationship with the still unborn but imaginable children. In other words, the given effect breeds a vague but quite disagreeable little cause which keeps moving like a worm in a raspberry, worrying us after the curtain has gone down. In examining this method I assume, of course, that the murder is a direct consequence of a previous conflict and in this sense it is easier to bring about than natural death. But, as I have explained, the murderer remains, and the effect is not final.

So we come to the third method, suicide. It can be used

either indirectly, with the murderer first killing the hero and then himself, so as to remove all traces of what is really the author's crime, or it can be used directly with the main character taking his own life. This again is easier to pull off than natural death, as it is rather plausible for a man, after a hopeless struggle with hopeless circumstances, to take his fate into his hands. No wonder, then, that of the three methods suicide is your determinist's favorite. But here a new and awful difficulty arises. Though a murder can be, *à la rigueur,* staged directly before our eyes, it is extraordinarily difficult to stage a good suicide. It was feasible in the old days, when such symbolic instruments as daggers and bodkins were used, but nowadays we can't very well show a man cutting his throat with a Gillette blade. Where poison is employed the agonies of the suicidee can be too horrible to watch, and are sometimes too lengthy, while the implication that the poison was so strong that the man just fell dead is somehow neither fair nor plausible. Generally speaking the best way out is the pistol shot, but it is impossible to *show* the actual thing—because, again, if treated in a plausible manner, it is apt to be too messy for the stage. Moreover, *any* suicide *on* the stage diverts the attention of the audience from the moral point or from the plot itself, exciting in us the pardonable interest with which we watch how an actor will proceed to kill himself plausibly and politely with the maximum of thoroughness and the minimum of bloodshed. Showmanship can certainly find many practical methods while actually leaving the actor on the stage, but, as I say, the more elaborate the thing is, the more our minds wander away from the inner spirit to the outer body of the dying actor—always assuming that it is an ordinary cause-and-effect play. We are left thus with only one possibility: the *backstage pistol-shot suicide.* And you will remember that, in stage directions, the author will generally describe this as a "muffled shot." Not a good loud bang, but "a muffled shot," so that sometimes there is an element of doubt among the characters on the stage regarding that sound, though the audience knows exactly what that sound was. And now comes a new and perfectly awful difficulty. Statistics—and statistics are the only regular income of your determinist, just as there are people who make a regular income out of careful gambling—show that, in real life, out of ten attempts at suicide by pistol shot, as many as three are abortive, leaving the subject alive; five result in a long agony; and *only two* bring on instant death. Thus, even if the characters do understand what happens, a mere muffled shot is insufficient to convince us that the man is really dead. The usual method, then, after the muffled shot has cooed its message, is to have a character investigate and then come back with the information that the man is dead. Now, except in the rare case when the investigator is a physician, the mere sentence "He is dead," or perhaps something "deeper" like, for instance, "He has paid his debt," is hardly convincing coming from a person who, it is assumed, is neither sufficiently learned nor sufficiently careless to wave aside any possibility, however vague, of bringing the victim back to life. If, on the other hand, the investigator comes back shrieking, "Jack has shot himself! Call a doctor at once!" and the final curtain goes down, we are left wondering whether, in our times of *patchable* hearts, a good physician might not save the mangled party. Indeed, the effect that is fondly supposed to be final may, beyond the play, start a young doctor of genius upon some stupendous career of life-saving. So, shall we wait for the doctor and see what he says and *then* ring down the curtain? Impossible—there is *no time* for further suspense; the man, whoever he is, has paid his debt and the play is over. The right way, then, is to add, after "debt," "It is too late to call a doctor"; that is, we introduce the word "doctor" as a kind of symbolic or masonic sign—not meaning, say, that we (the messenger) are sufficiently learned and sufficiently unsentimental to know that no doctor will help, but conveying to the audience by a conventional sign, by this rapid "doctor" sound, something that stresses the positive finality of the effect. But actually there is no way of making the suicide quite, quite final, unless, as I said, the herald himself be a doctor. So we come to the very curious conclusion that a really ironclad tragedy, with no possible chink in cause or effect—that is, the ideal play that textbooks teach people to write and theatrical managers clamor for—that this masterpiece, whatever its plot or background, 1) *must* end in suicide, 2) *must* contain *one character at least* who is a doctor, 3) that this doctor must be a *good doctor* and, 4) that it is he who must find the body. In other words, from the mere fact of tragedy's being what it is we have deduced an actual play. And this is the tragedy of tragedy.

In speaking of this technique, I have begun at the end of a modern tragedy to show what it must aspire to if it wants to be quite, quite consistent. Actually, the plays you may remember do not conform to such strict canons, and thus are not only bad in themselves, but do not even trouble to render plausible the bad rules they follow. For, numerous other conventions are unavoidably bred by the causal convention. We may hastily examine some of these.

A more sophisticated form of the French "dusting the furniture" exposition is when, instead of the valet and the maid discovered onstage, we have two visitors *arriving* on the stage as the curtain is going up, speaking of what brought them, and of the people in the house. It is a pathetic attempt to comply with the request of critics and teachers who demand that the exposition coincide with action, and actually the *entrance* of two visitors is action. But why on earth should two people who arrived on the same train and who had ample time to discuss everything during the journey, why must they struggle to keep silent till the minute of arrival, whereupon they start talking of their hosts in the wrongest place imaginable—the parlor of the house where they are guests? Why? Because the author must have them explode right here with a time-bomb exposition.

The next trick, to take the most obvious ones, is the promise of somebody's arrival. So-and-so is expected. We know that so-and-so will unavoidably come. He or she will come very soon. In fact he or she comes a minute after it has been said that the arrival will occur perhaps after dinner, perhaps tomorrow morning (which is meant to divert the audience's attention from the rapidity of the apparition: "Oh, I took an earlier train" is the usual explanation). If, when promising the audience a visitor, the speaker remarks that by the by so-and-so is coming—this *by the by* is a pathetic means of concealing the fact that so-and-so will play a most important, if not *the* most important, part in the play. Indeed, more often than not the "by and by" brings in the so-called fertilizing character. These promises, being links in the iron chain of tragic causation, are inevitably kept. The so-called *scène à faire*, the obligatory scene, is not, as most critics seem to think, *one* scene in the play—it is really every *next* scene in the play, no matter how ingenious the author may be in the way of surprises, or rather *just because* he is expected to surprise. A cousin from Australia is mentioned; somehow or other the characters expect him to be a grumpy old bachelor; now, the audience is not particularly eager to meet a grumpy old bachelor; but the cousin from Australia turns out to be the bachelor's fascinating young niece. The arrival is an obligatory scene because any intelligent audience had vaguely expected the author to make some amends for promising a bore. This example refers certainly more to comedy than to tragedy, but analogous methods are employed in the most serious plays: for example, in Soviet tragedies where more often than not the expected commissar turns out to be a slip of a girl—and then this slip of a girl turns out to be an expert with a revolver when another character turns out to be a bourgeois Don Juan in disguise.

Among modern tragedies there is *one* that ought to be studied particularly closely by anyone wishing to find *all* the disastrous results of cause and effect, neatly grouped together in one play. This is O'Neill's *Mourning Becomes Electra.* Just as the weather changed according to human moods and moves in Ibsen's play, here, in *Mourning Becomes Electra,* we observe the curious phenomenon of a young woman who is flat-chested in the first act, becomes a full-bosomed beautiful creature after a trip to the South Islands, then, *a couple of days later,* reverts to the original flat-chested, sharp-elbowed type. We have a couple of suicides of the wildest sort, and the *positive-finality* trick is supplied by the heroine's telling us just before the play ends that she will not commit suicide, but will go on living in the dismal house, etc., though there is nothing to prevent her changing her mind, and using the same old army pistol so conveniently supplied to the other patients of the play. Then there is the element of Fate, Fate whom the author leads by one hand, and the late professor Freud by the other. There are portraits on the wall, dumb creatures, which are used for the purpose of monologue under the queer misconception that a monologue becomes a dialogue if the portrait of another person is addressed. There are many such interesting things in this play. But perhaps the most remarkable thing, one that throws direct light on the inevitable artificial side of tragedies based on the logic of fate, is the difficulties the author experiences in keeping this or that character on the stage when he is especially required, but when some pathetic flaw in the machinery suggests that the really natural thing would be a hasty retreat. For instance: the old gentleman of tragedy is expected to return from the war tomorrow or possibly after tomorrow, which means that he arrives almost immediately after the beginning of the act with the usual explanation about trains. It is late in the evening. The evening is cold. The only place to sit is the steps of the porch. The old gentleman is tired, hungry, has not been home for ages and moreover suffers from acute heart trouble—a pain like a knife, he says, which is meant to prepare his death in another act. Now the horrible job with which the author is faced is to make that poor old man remain in the bleak garden, on the damp steps, for a good talk with his daughter and his wife—especially with his wife. The casual reasons for his not going into the house, which are inserted here and there in the talk, keep excluding one another in a most fascinating way—and the tragedy of the act is not the tragedy of the old man's relations with his wife, but the tragedy of an honest, tired, hungry, helpless human being, grimly held by the author who, until the act is over, keeps him away from bath, slippers and supper.

The peculiar technique of this play and of other plays by other authors is not so much the result of poor talent, as the unavoidable result of the illusion that life and thus dramatic art picturing life should be based on a steady current of cause and effect driving us towards the ocean of death. The themes, the ideas of tragedies have certainly changed, but the change is unfortunately just the change in an actor's dressing room, mere new disguises that only *appear* new, but whose interplay is always the same: conflict between this and that, and then the same iron rules of conflict leading either to a happy or miserable end, but always to *some* end which is unavoidably *contained* in the cause. Nothing ever fizzles out in a tragedy, though perhaps one of the tragedies of life is that even the most tragic situations just fizzle out. Anything remotely resembling an accident is taboo. The conflicting characters are not live people, but types—and this is especially noticeable in the absurd though well-meant plays, which are supposed to depict—if not to solve—the tragedy of the present times. In such plays what I call the *island* or *Grand Hotel* or *Magnolia Street* method is used, that is, the grouping of people in a dramatically convenient, strictly limited space with either social tradition or some outside calamity preventing their dispersal. In such tragedies the old German refugee, though otherwise fairly stolid, will invariably love music, the Russian émigré woman will be a fascinating vamp and rave about Tsars and the snow, the Jew will be married to a Christian, the spy will be blond and bland, and the young married couple naive and pathetic— and so on and on—and no matter where you group them it is always the same old story (even the transatlantic Clipper has been tried, and certainly nobody heeded the critics who humbly asked what engineering device had been used to eliminate the roar of the propellers). The conflict of ideas replacing the conflict of passion changes *nothing* in the essential pattern—if anything, it makes it still more artificial. Hobnobbing with the audience through the medium of a chorus has been tried, only resulting in the destruction of the main and fundamental agreement on which stage drama can be based. This agreement is: we are aware of the characters on the stage, but cannot move them; they are unaware of us, but can move us—a perfect division which, when tampered with, transforms plays into what they are today.

The Soviet tragedies are in fact the last word in the cause-and-effect pattern, plus something that the bourgeois stage is helplessly groping for: a good machine god that will do away with the need to search for a plausible final effect.

This god, coming inevitably at the end of Soviet tragedy and indeed regulating the whole play, is none other than the *idea of the perfect state* as understood by communists. I do not wish to imply that what irritates me here is propaganda. In fact, I don't see why if, say, one type of theatre may indulge in patriotic propaganda or democratic propaganda another cannot indulge in communist propaganda, or in any other kind of propaganda.

I don't see any difference because, perhaps, all kinds of propaganda leave me perfectly cold whether their subject appeals to me or not. But what I do mean is that whenever propaganda is contained in a play the determinist chain is drawn still tighter around the throat of the tragic muse. In Soviet tragedies, moreover, we get a special kind of dualism which makes them well-nigh unbearable—in book form at least. The wonders of staging and acting that have been preserved in Russia since the nineties of the last century, when the Art Theatre appeared, can certainly make entertainment even out of the lowest trash. The dualism to which I refer, and which is the most typical and remarkable feature of the Soviet drama, consists in the following: We know and Soviet authors know that the dialectical idea of any Soviet tragedy *must* be that party emotions, emotions related to the worship of the State, are above ordinary human or bourgeois feeling, so that any form of moral or physical cruelty, if and when it leads to the triumph of Socialism, is admissible. On the other hand, because the play must be good melodrama, in order to attract popular fancy, there is a kind of queer agreement that *certain* actions may *not* be performed even by the most consistent Bolshevik— such as cruelty to children or betrayal of a friend; that is, mingled with the most traditional heroics of all times, we find the rosiest sentimentalities of old-fashioned fiction. So that, in the long run, the most extreme form of leftist theatre, notwithstanding its healthy looks and dynamic harmonies, is really a reversion to the most primitive and hackneyed forms of literature.

I would not wish, however, to create the impression that, if I fail to be spiritually excited by modern drama, I deny it all value. As a matter of fact, here and there, in Strindberg, in Chekhov, in Shaw's brilliant farces (especially *Candida*), in at least one Galsworthy play (for instance, *Strife*), in one or two French plays (for instance, Lenormand's *Time Is a Dream*), in one or two American plays such as the first act of *The Children's Hour* and the first act of *Of Mice and Men* (the rest of the play is dismal nonsense)—in many existing plays, there are indeed magnificent bits, artistically rendered emotions and, most important, that special atmosphere which is the sign that the author has freely created a world of his own. But the perfect tragedy has not yet been produced.

The idea of conflict tends to endow life with a logic it never has. Tragedies based exclusively on the logic of conflict are as untrue to life as an all-pervading class-struggle idea is untrue to history. Most of the worst and deepest human tragedies, far from following the marble rules of tragic conflict, are tossed on the stormy element of chance. This element of chance playwrights have so completely excluded from their dramas that any denouement due to an earthquake or to an automobile accident strikes the audience as incongruous if, naturally, the earthquake has not been expected all along or the automobile has not been a dramatic investment from the very start. The life of a tragedy is, as it were, too short for accidents to happen; but at the same time tradition demands that life on the stage develop according to rules—the rules of passionate conflict—rules whose rigidity is at least as ridiculous as the stumblings of chance. What even the greatest playwrights have never realized is that chance is not always stumbling and that the tragedies of real life are based on the beauty or horror of chance—not merely on its ridiculousness. And it is this secret rhythm of chance that one would like to see pulsating in the veins of the tragic muse. Otherwise, if only the rules of conflict and fate and divine justice and imminent death are followed, tragedy is limited both by its platform and by its unswerving doom, and becomes in the long run a hopeless scuffle—the scuffle between a condemned man and the executioner. But life is not a scaffold, as tragic playwrights tend to suggest. I have so seldom been moved by the tragedy I have seen or read because I could never believe in the ridiculous laws that they presupposed. The charm of tragic genius, the charm of Shakespeare or Ibsen, lies for me in quite another region.

What then ought tragedy to be if I deny it what is considered its most fundamental characteristic—conflict ruled by the causal laws of human fate? First of all I doubt the real existence of these laws in the simple and severe form that the stage has adopted. I doubt that any strict line can be drawn between the tragic and the burlesque, fatality and chance, causal subjection and the caprice of free will. What seems to me to be the higher form of tragedy is the creation of a certain unique pattern of life in which the sorrows and passing of a particular man will follow the rules of his own individuality, not the rules of the theatre as we know them. It would be absurd to suggest, however, that accident and chance may be left to play havoc with life on the stage. But it is not absurd to say that a writer of genius may discover exactly the right harmony of such accidental occurrences, and that this harmony, without suggesting anything like the iron laws of tragic fatality, will express certain definite combinations that occur in life. And it is high time, too, for playwrights to forget the notions that they must please the audience and that this audience is a collection of half-wits;

that plays, as one writer on the subject solemnly asserts, must never contain anything important in the first ten minutes, because, you see, late dinners are the fashion; and that every important detail must be repeated so that even the least intelligent spectator will at last grasp the idea. The only audience that a playwright must imagine is the ideal one, that is, *himself.* All the rest pertains to the box-office, not to dramatic art.

"That's all very fine," said the producer leaning back in his armchair and puffing on the cigar which fiction assigns to his profession, "that's all very fine—but business is business, so how can you expect plays based on some new technique which will make them unintelligible to the general public, plays not only departing from tradition, but flaunting their disregard for the wits of the audience, tragedies which arrogantly reject the causal fundamentals of the particular form of dramatic art that they represent—how can you expect such plays to be produced by any big theatre company?" Well, I don't—and this, too, is the tragedy of tragedy.